Thomas Anburey

Travels through the interior parts of America

In a series of letters

Thomas Anburey

Travels through the interior parts of America
In a series of letters

ISBN/EAN: 9783742842435

Manufactured in Europe, USA, Canada, Australia, Japa

Cover: Foto ©Andreas Hilbeck / pixelio.de

Manufactured and distributed by brebook publishing software (www.brebook.com)

Thomas Anburey

Travels through the interior parts of America

TRAVELS

THROUGH THE

INTERIOR PARTS

OF

AMERICA.

IN A

SERIES OF LETTERS.

BY AN OFFICER.

Τί ἂν, ἂν τις εἴποι, ταῦτα λίγεις ἡμῖν νυν;
Ἵνα γνῶτε, καὶ αἰσθῆσθε ἀμφότερα.
DEMOSTH. OLYNTH.

VOL. I.

LONDON:
Printed for WILLIAM LANE, Leadenhall-Street.
MDCCLXXXIX.

TO THE RIGHT HONORABLE THE

EARL OF HARRINGTON,

VISCOUNT PETERSHAM,

AND

COLONEL OF THE TWENTY-NINTH REGIMENT OF FOOT.

MY LORD,

HAVING had the honor to serve under your Lordship, it was my fortune, in common with all who were in the same situa-

situation, to become attached to your Lordship by personal obligations; and it is a consequence which I hope will be thought equally natural, that I should take this occasion to acknowledge them.

In laying before the Public uncommon scenes of difficulty, danger and distress, I might be further tempted, had I talents for the undertaking, to particularize the unremitting fortitude, which, in several of the most trying instances, distinguished your Lordship's conduct: but examples of bravery, though none can be more conspicuous than those your Lordship shewed, abound in every class of a British army: more rare though

though not less worthy of imitation, is the sort of attachment your Lordship has always shewn to your corps.

It has been your praise, my Lord, when out of the field, to forego the pleasures which high rank, fortune, youth, and accomplishments opened to your view, and to brave the severity of climate, through tedious winters, in mere military fellowship.

In retired quarters, you found the care of your men to be at once the true preparation for your country's service, and a most gratifying enjoyment to your own benevolence: while on their parts, they

they considered their leader as their best friend and benefactor. Discipline was thus placed upon a basis that mechanical valor can never establish, upon a principle worthy of troops who can think and feel, *confidence* and *gratitude.*

Duly impressed with these and many other of your virtues---many more than you would permit me to enumerate; I have the honor to be

My Lord,

Your Lordship's most obedient,

And most devoted

Humble Servant,

THOMAS ANBUREY.

PREFACE.

THE following letters were written to gratify private friendſhip, and would never have been intruded upon the Public, but from the entreaties of ſome of the moſt reſpectable Subſcribers to the Work, who flattered the Author, that as they contained much authentic information, relative to America, little known on this ſide of the Atlantic, they could not fail of being intereſting to the Public.

Their

Their style and manner will clearly evince them to be the actual result of a familiar correspondence, and by no means void of those inaccuracies necessarily arising from the rapid effusions of a confessedly inexperienced Writer, which will scarcely be wondered at, by those who consider how widely different are the qualifications necessary to form the Soldier and the Author.

Every thing the Reader may meet with will not appear strictly *nouvelle*; but this is a circumstance unavoidably attending the writer of a tour through a country, which has been already the subject of so much discussion; but there are certainly many new circumstances related, which will serve to point out the true character and manners of the Americans.

The facts came within his own knowledge, or are supported by some honourable authority; and his motto has ever been,

*———Nothing extenuate,
Nor set down aught in Malice.*

They will strike every man with the greater force, after the evident partiality of a late Author, who has been led to represent the Favorers of Independence as possessed of every amiable qualification, and those who espoused the rights of the Mother Country, as destitute of common feelings, and humanity itself.

The Author, sensible how much those Subscribers, whose generosity has exceeded the limits of the subscription, would be hurt by a particular distinction, co-jointly renders them those thanks,

" Which the tried heart that feels alone can give."

DIRECTIONS FOR PLACING THE PLATES.

VOL. I.

	Facing Page
Map of America, opposite the Title Page	
View of St. John's, upon the River Sorrell	136
The Section and Plan of a Blockhouse	138
Indian Warrior	291
View of the Blockhouse and Saw Mill	350
View of the Encampment at Still Water	433

VOL. II.

American Continental Dollars	400
View of the Encampment of the Convention Army, at Charlottesville	443

SUBSCRIBERS

TO

THE WORK.

HIS ROYAL HIGHNESS—THE DUKE OF YORK
HIS ROYAL HIGHNESS—PRINCE WILLIAM HENRY
HIS ROYAL HIGHNESS—THE DUKE OF GLOUCESTER
HIS ROYAL HIGHNESS—THE DUKE OF CUMBERLAND

A

His Grace———The Duke of Argyle
The Right Hon.———The Earl of Altamont
The Right Hon.———Lord Audley
The Hon. Lady———Harriet Ackland
His Excellency———Baron D'Alvensleben

THE ROYAL REGIMENT OF ARTILLERY:

Lieut. Col. Walker
————Johnston

Major Williams
———— Lemoine
———— Blomefield
Captain Houghton
————— Dyfart
—————Willington
—————Whitworth
—————Collier
—————Remington
—————Howarth
—————Hadden
Lieut. Reed
———— Neville
———— Sutton
Surgeon Mr. Wild

Major Affleck,————Portland-Street
Capt. Armstrong, (8 Regt. of Foot)
James Abel, Efq.————Cloak-Lane
John Adams, Efq.
Alexander Adair, Efq.————Pall Mall
Mrs. Towers Allen,—Queen's-Square
Mr. A. C. Arnold,————Loweftoff
Mr. Rd. Aldridge,————Briftol
Mr. Wm. Auftin,————Idol-Lane
Ainfley's Library,————Edinburgh
Andrews's Library, ————Worcefter
Mr. Axtell,———— Cornhill
James P. Andrews, Efq.
Amicable Society,————Northampton

B

The Rt. Hon.————The Earl of Buckinghamfhire
The Rt. Hon.————The Earl of Barrymore
The Rt. Hon.————The Earl of Balcarres
The Rt. Hon.————The Countefs of Balcarres
The Rt. Hon.————The Earl of Breadalbane
The Rt. Hon.————Vifcount Barrington
The Rt. Hon.————Vifcount Beauchamp
The Rt. Hon.————Lord Brownlow

SUBSCRIBERS

—— Braddyll, Esq.
Mrs. Braddyll
Sir Robert Barker, Bart.
Sir William Augustus Brown, Bart.
Richard Benyon, Esq. M. P.
General Burgoyne
Dr. Brocklesby, ——Norfolk-Street
Lieut. Col. Bowyer, (66 Regt.)
Capt. Bell, (19 Regt.)
Lieut. Col. Baillie, ——Edinburgh
Capt. Bowen, Independent Comp.
Capt. Barrette, ——Doncaster, (100 Regt.)
Lieut. Budworth, (72 Regt.)
Richard Barwell, Esq. M. P.
—— Blomfield, Esq.
John Bax, Esq.——Preston, Kent
John Benjafield, Esq.—— Parliament-Street
Thomas Beardmore, Esq.——Temple
Mr. John Berry,——Canterbury-Square
The Rev. Mr. Bowcher,——Piccadilly
George Biggins, Esq. ——Essex-Street
Ynyr Burgess, Esq.——East India House
The Rev. Dr. Bate,——Walton
Lieut. Bartlet, (Royal Engineers)——Chatham
Mr. Broughton,——Treasury
Mr. John Breadhower,——Portsmouth
Mr. Barnikle,——Plymouth
Mr. Burtenshaw's Library,——Brighthelmstone
Thomas Bowes, Esq.
Mr. Bull's Library, —— Bath
Mr. Thomas Batchelor,——Bristol
Mr. Beazeley,——Black-Friars Road
Mr. J. B. Becket,——Bristol
John Bourchier, Esq.——Ipswich
Mr. Barrukel
Rob. Barrett, Esq.——London
Capt. Arthur Buttell,——Marines
James Betts, Esq.——Essex-Street
Wm. Butler, Esq.——Gresse-Street
Mr. Baker's Library,——Southampton
Mr. Barry's Library, ——Hastings

SUBSCRIBERS.

C

The Rt. Hon.——The Earl of Chesterfield
The Rt. Hon.——The Earl of Carlisle
The Rt. Hon.——The Earl of Cholmondeley
The Rt. Hon.——The Earl of Camden
The Rt. Hon.——The Earl of Cavan
The Rt. Hon.——Lord Craven
The Rt. Hon.——Lord Clifford
The Rt. Hon.——Lord Carberry
The Rt. Hon.——Lord Cathcart
The Rt. Hon.——Lord Fred. Campbell
Sir Wm. Clerke, Bart.
Sir Hy. Gough Calthorpe,
Sir Henry Clinton, K. B.
General Christie,——Leicester-Square
Major Campbell, (24 Regt. of Foot)
Capt. Cotter, (103 Regt.)
Bryan Cooke, Esq.
Mrs. Cooke
Wm. Cowden, Esq.——Meuse
Ralph Clayton, Esq.
Richard Crofts, Esq.——Pall Mall
The Rev. Mr. Cove,——Helstone
Mrs. Casement,——ditto
James Crowdy, Esq.——Swindon, Wilts
Mr. Jos. Colborne, Surgeon,——Brentwood
Mr. Edm. Cotterell,——Cold Bath Fields
Mr. James Cooper,——Swithin's-Lane
Dr. Cockall
Mr. Thomas Conder,——Aldersgate Street
The Rev. Mr. Crutwell,——Oakingham
James Cobb, Esq.——East India House
Mr. Crawford's Library,——Brighthelmstone
Jos. Chew, Esq Sec. for India Affairs,——North America
William Curtis, Esq.——London
Lieut. Crichton, (31 Regt.)——Gosport
J. Croft, Esq.

SUBSCRIBERS.

D

His Grace——The Duke of Devonshire
The Rt. Hon.——The Earl of Derby
The Rt. Hon.——The Earl of Dartmouth
The Rt. Hon.——The Earl of Donegal
The Rt. Hon.——The Countess of Darnley
The Rt. Hon.——Viscount Duncannon
The Rt. Hon.——Viscount Dalrymple
The Rt. Hon.——Lord Ducie
The Rt. Hon.——Lord Dorchester
Colonel Dundas
Lieut. Will. Dalton, (Royal Navy)——Rotherhithe
Lieut. Col. Delancey, Margaret-Street, Cavendish-Square
Major Dalrymple, (49 Regt. of Foot)
Capt. Duncan
Richard Dowding, Esq.——Shadwell
Mr. George Dixon,——Wooburne
Mr. John Dew,——Shenfield
Mr. B. U. Dowson,——Geldeston
The Rev. D. Davies,——Macclesfield
Dulot and Owen's Library,——Brighthelmstone
Mess. Downes and March,——Yarmouth
The Rev. H. Bate Dudley, Bradwell
Rich. Jles Dimsdale, Esq.

E

The Rt. Hon.——The Earl of Effingham
The Rt. Hon.——The Earl of Eglintoune
The Rt. Hon.——The Earl of Eufton
The Rt. Hon.——Lord Elphinstone
Sir James Erskine, Bart.——Cavendish-Square

THE ROYAL ENGINEERS.

Major General Sir William Greene, Bart.
Lieut. Col. Moncrief
Capt. Twiss

Capt. Rudyard
Lieut. Beatson
—— Courture
—— Bartlett
Mrs. Edgar,——Percy-Street
Mrs. Edwards,——Savage-Gardens
Mr. Thomas Evans,——Minories

F

The Rt. Hon.——The Earl of Falconberg
The Rt. Hon.——Viscount Falmouth
The Rt. Hon.——Viscount Fielding
The Rt. Hon.——Charles James Fox
The Rt. Hon.——M. Fitzpatrick

FIRST (OR KING's) REGIMENT OF DRAGOON GUARDS.

General Sir George Howard, K. B.
Lieut. Col. Vyse
Capt. Trotter
Lieut. Hawley
—— Syer
—— Beckford
—— Serjeantson
—— Need
Cornet Hamilton

FIRST REGIMENT OF FOOT GUARDS.

Colonel Bertie
—— Strickland
—— Hon. Francis Needham
—— Hon. H. F. Stanhope
—— Sir Charles Asgill, Bart.

FIFTEENTH REGIMENT OF FOOT.

Lieut. Gen. Sir. Wm. Fawcett
Lieut. Col. Myers

SUBSCRIBERS.

Capt. Madden
—— Ditmas
—— Paumier
—— Spencer
—— Gordon
—— Brown
—— Cockburne
Lieut. Ball
————Stopford
Enfign Barnard
———— Mc Donald
Qr. Mafter Watkins
Surgeon Mr. Anderfon

FORTY-SIXTH REGIMENT OF FOOT,

Lieut. Col. Hon. Colin Lindfay
Major Leighton
Capt. Bell
—— Wale
Lieut. Lloyd
————James
————Dallas

FORTY-SEVENTH REGIMENT OF FOOT,

Lieut. Col. Irving
Major Coote
————Alcock
————Aubrey
Capt. Sir Henry Mart
—— Featherftone
Lieut. Johnfon
————Hill
————Baldwin
————Mc Lean

FORTY-EIGHTH REGIMENT OF FOOT.

Lieut. Col. Hedges
Major D'Arcy

Major Campbell
Capt. Jones
Lieut. Jones
—— Roberts
Enſign Beevor
———— Power

Colonel Forbes,————Arlington-Street
Lieut. Col. Forſter, (66 Regt. Foot)
Thomas Forſyth, Eſq.————New Bond-Street
Cuthbert Fiſher, Eſq.————Tower
J. Flint, Eſq.————Shrewſbury
Mr. Fletcher,————Liverpool 2 ſets
Mr. Forreſt,————St. Martin's-Lane
Roſe Fuller, Eſq.————Wigmore-Street
Walter Farquhar, Eſq.————Great Marlborough-Street
Mr. Firmin,————Strand
Thomas Fortune, Eſq.————London
Mr. Fenno's Library,————Colcheſter

G

His Grace————The Duke of Grafton
His Grace————The Duke of Gordon
The Rt. Hon.————Earl Groſvenor
The Rt. Hon.————Earl of Glaſgow
The Rt. Hon.————Lord Gage
General Gordon
Capt. Gwynn
Lieut. Gordon,————Parliament-Street
———— Grant, Eſq.
Richard Gray, Eſq.————Pall Mall
Mrs. Gibſon,————Hertford-Street
Samuel Greaves, Eſq.————Mancheſter
The Rev. Mr. Gryll,————Helſtone
Mr. T. Gryll,   ditto
Thomas Glynn, Eſq.
The Rev. Mr. Gilbert,————Helſtone
Mr. Gardner,————London

SUBSCRIBERS.

H

His Grace————The Duke of Hamilton
The Rt. Hon.————The Earl of Huntingdon
The Rt. Hon.————The Earl of Harrington
The Rt. Hon.————The Earl of Harcourt
The Rt. Hon.————The Earl of Hertford
The Rt. Hon.————Lord Howard
The Rt. Hon.————Lord Hawke
The Rt. Hon.————Lord Hawkesbury
The Rt. Hon.————Lord Heathfield
The Rt. Hon.————Lord Hood
The Rt. Hon.————Lord Archibald Hamilton
The Rt. Hon.————Lord Spencer Hamilton
Sir Watts Horton, Bart.
The Hon. Mrs. Horton
The Hon. Lady Horton
The Rev. Mr. Horton
The Hon. Mr. Heneage
Mr. Harman, Princes-Street, opposite the Mansion-House

THE ROYAL REGIMENT OF HORSE GUARDS.

The Rt. Hon.————General Conway
Col. Balthwayt
Capt. Milnes
———— Chaplin
———— Jefferson

Col. Harnage,————Parliament-Street
Major Hawker,————ditto
Capt. Hanchett
Capt. Hardy
Major Haines,————Hampshire
Mr. Hall, Surgeon, (51 Regt.)
The Rev. Mr. Hornby
Mrs. Hindes,————Hertford-Street
John Hawkins, Esq.————Helstone
James Watson Hull, Esq.————Belvedere, Ireland

SUBSCRIBERS.

Trevor Hull, Esq. ———Greek-Street
Mr. Hinckes,———Great Portland-Street
Mr. John Harding,———Strand
Mr Hollyoake,——— Red Lion-Square
Mr. Harris,——— St. Mary Axe
Anthony Highmore, Esq. ditto
Edward Heylin, Esq ———Islington
Mr. Hope,———Upper Seymour-Street, Cavendish-Square
Benj. Henshaw, Esq ———Hodsdon
Thomas Hodgson, Esq ———Bristol
Mess. Haydon and Sons,———Plymouth
The Gentlemens Book Club———at Helstone.
Col. Hill, (late of the 9th Regt.)———Helstone
Capt. Richard Hill, ———Helstone
William Hoste, Esq. Barwick
Mr. George Hall,——— Star-Office, Exeter-Street

I

The Rt. Hon. ———The Earl of Jersey
Lieut. Col. Jacques, (51. Regt. of Foot)
Sir John Johnson, Superintendant to the Indians in Canada
Col. Jessop,———Fludyer-Street
Lieut. Jones,———Lower Brook-Street
Gen. Johnson
Alex. Irvine, Esq.———Berner's-Street
Mr. Richard Johns,———Helstone
Mr. Johnson,———Piccadilly
Mr. Samuel Johnson,———Bristol

K

The Rt. Hon.———Lord Kensington
Lieut. Col. Kingston, (28 Regt, of Foot)
Capt. Kempthorne,———Helstone
——— Kellett, Esq.———Russel-Street, Covent-Garden
John Keene, Esq.———Mansion House
Mr. James Kerby,———London
Mr. Charles Knight,———Windsor
Mr. Frederic Kanmacher

SUBSCRIBERS.

L

His Grace ———— The Duke of Leeds
The Rt. Hon. ———— The Marquifs of Lanfdown
The Rt. Hon ———— The Marquifs of Lothain
The Rt Hon. ———— The Earl Ludlow
The Rt. Hon. ———— Lord Lovaine
The Hon. ———— Robert Lindfay
The Hon. ———— Capt. John Lindfay
The Hon ———— Hugh Lindfay
Sir Michael Le Fleming, Bart. ———— Hertford-Street
General Lambton, ———— Harley-Street
Paul Le Mefurier, Efq. — M.P. — Walbrook
Charter Layton, Efq. ———— Drayton
Mr. Loxley, ———— Poultry
Mr. Lofack, ———— Wigmore-Street
Mr. John Lee, ———— Black-Friars
Mr. Leigh, ———— Thorndon
Mr. John Lees, ———— Brentford

M

His Grace ———— The Duke of Marlborough
His Grace ———— The Duke of Montrofe
The Rt. Hon. ———— Vifcount Mount Edgecumbe
The Rt. Hon. ———— Vifcount Molefworth
The Rt. Hon. ———— Vifcount Melbourne
The Rt. Hon. ———— Vifcount Mountftuart
The Rt. Hon. ———— Lord Milford
Richard Mafter, Efq M P. — Charles-Street, BerkleyqSq.
J. Madocks, Efq. (Coldftream Regt. Gds.) Bedford-Street
Major Money, ———— Norwich
Capt. Mc. Kinnon, ———— (63 Regt.) Ireland
Capt. Robert Mc. Crea, ———— Guernfey
Cuthbert Mafhiter, Efq. ———— Romford
Edward Mafon, Efq. ———— Spital-Fields
The Rev. Mr. Mingin, ———— Golden-Square
Mr. Mackreth, ———— Scotland-Yard
Mr. Jofeph Mitchell, ———— Hel!lone
J. Milbanke, Efq.

SUBSCRIBERS.

The Rev. Dr. Morgan,——St. James's-Square
James Madden, Efq.——St. Albans-Street
Thomas Maude, Efq.——Temple
Mr. Mc Leifh's Library, Edinburgh

N

His Grace——The Duke of Northumberland

THE NINTH REGIMENT OF FOOT.

Lieut. Col. Campbell
Major Ritchie
Capt. Baillie
—— Hoey
—— Buchannan
—— Spencer
—— Vincent
—— Timms
—— Murray
—— Piercy
—— Rofe
—— Mc Lean
Lieut. Reynolds
——Mitchell
—— Fatio
Enfigns James Rofe
—— Duffe
—— Dalziel
—— Burbridge
—— O'Connor
Enfign Keightley
—— Wolfe
Chaplain—The Rev. Mr. Clewlow

THE ROYAL NAVY.

Admiral Montague
Capt. Dacres

SUBSCRIBERS.

—— Hardy
—— Schanks
Lieut. Wm. Dalton
—— Wm. Bentick
Mrs. Newberry,——St. Paul's Church-Yard

O

Sir George Osborn, Bart. Charles-Street, Berkley-Square
James Ormsby, Esq.——Dublin

P

His Grace——The Duke of Portland
Her Grace——The Dutchess of Portland
The Rt. Hon.——The Earl of Plymouth
The Rt. Hon.——The Earl of Powis
The Rt. Hon.——Viscount Palmerstone
The Rt. Hon.——Lord Pelham
The Rt. Hon.——Lord Petre
The Hon.——Mr. Petre, Grosvenor-Square
The Hon.——Mr. G. Petre, Somerset-Street
The Hon.——Thomas Pelham, Stretton-Street
The Hon.——General Parker
Gen. Pitt,——Tenterden-Street
Capt. Peacock,——(17 Regt. of Foot)
Mr. Pugh,——Poultry
Mrs. Piozzi,——Hanover-Square
Mr. Phillips, Somersetshire
Mr. Thomas Powell,——Terace, Buckingham-Street
Mr. Parnell,——Church-Street, Spital-Fields
Capt. Walter Proffer,——Ireland
Palmer and Merrick's Library,——Oxford
Mr. Powell,——Newgate-Street
Punchard and Jermyns's Library, Ipswich
Thomas Boothby Parkyns, Esq.
Thomas Paulk, Esq.

SUBSCRIBERS.

R

The Rt. Hon. ———The Earl of Radnor
The Rt. Hon. ———Lord Rivers
The Rt. Hon. ———Lord Rodney
The Rt. Hon. ———Lord Rawdon
Sir Matthew White Ridley, Bart. ———Portland-Place
Capt. Reed,——— (103 Regt.)
Mr. Robson,———Princes-Street, Hanover-Square
Mr. Alexander Roberts,———Red Lion-Square
John Rogers, Esq.———Helstone
E. Read, Esq. Chester
George Rome, Esq. Mount-Street
John Le Chevalier Roome, Esq.———London-Road
Mr. Rush,———Fountain-Street
Alexander Raby, Esq.———Cobham
Mrs. Raby
Mr. Robinson,———Cornhill

S

His Grace———The Duke of St. Albans
The Rt. Hon.———The Earl of Suffolk
The Rt. Hon.———The Earl of Shaftesbury
The Rt. Hon.———The Countess Dow. of Shaftesbury
The Rt. Hon.———The Earl of Scarborough
The Rt. Hon.———The Earl of Stanhope
The Rt. Hon.———Earl Spencer
The Rt. Hon.———The Earl Stamford
The Rt. Hon.———Viscount Stormont
The Rt. Hon.———Lord Say and Sele
The Rt. Hon.———Lord Stourton
The Rt. Hon.———Lord St. John
The Rt. Hon.———Lord Scarsdale
The Rt. Hon.———Lord Southampton
The Rt. Hon.———Lord Robert Spencer
The Rt. Hon———Lady Ann Simpson
The Hon.——— ——— Mr. Sandilands
Thomas Stanley, Esq. M. P.———Pall Mall
R. B. Sheridan, Esq. M.P. ——— Bruton Street

SUBSCRIBERS.

SECOND (OR ROYAL N. BRITISH) REGT. OF DRAGOONS.

Major Ramsay
Capt. Seaford
—— Smith
—— Boardman
Lieut. Fortescue
Cornet Wigley
———— Bothwell
———— Leigh

SIXTEENTH (OR QUEEN'S) REGT. OF LIGHT DRAGOONS.

The Hon.——Major General Harcourt
Major Gardner
———— *Hon.* H. Bennett
———— Howell
Capt. Boyce
—— Carmichael
Lieut. Hawker
————Smallett
————Archer
————Munro
Cornet Ashton
——Lee
————Pennyman
Cornet Anson
————Deering

SIXTY-SECOND REGIMENT OF FOOT.

Major Gen.—Matthews
Lieut. Col. — Campbell
Major Howe
Capt. Banbury
—— Sotheron
—— Wybrants
—— Blackall

—— Matthias
—— Bromhead
—— Blacker
—— Vallancey
Lieut. James
—— Brudenell
—— Gourlay
—— Batchelor
—— Kerr
Enſign Kent
—— Garden

Major Skene,——Chelſea
Lieut. Stuart
Mr. Seddon,——Alderſgate-Street
John Sawrey, Eſq.——Lancaſhire
Edw. Spike, Eſq.
Mrs. Spike
Miſs Spike
Mr. John Slade,—— Camberwell
Daniel Seton, Eſq.——Stratford-Place
Mr. Shiercliffe,——Briſtol
Mr. Charles Spitta,——College-Hill
John Scott, Eſq.——Wigmore-Street
Capt. Scott, ——(53 Regt of Foot)
Mr. Scott, Jun.——Norwich
Miſs Smiths,——Percy-Street
James Simmonds, Eſq. Banker,——Canterbury
Simmons and Kirby, Canterbury
John Seleer, Eſq.——London
Mr. Stalker,——London
Mr. Sollors,——Blandford
The Rev. Mr. Salmon
Mr. J. F. Souel,——Guernſey
John Secker, Eſq.——Windſor
Stell's Library,——Haſtings

SUBSCRIBERS.

T

The Rt. Hon. ———The Marquifs of Titchfield
The Rt. Hon.———Lord Torphichen
The Hon.———Mr. Twifleton Thompfon
Sir Charles Thompfon, Bart. K.B. Bond-Street
Sir John Thorold, Bart.———Cavendifh-Square

THE THIRD REGIMENT OF HORSE, OR CARBINEERS.

Colonel Longfield
Major Wilford
———Willey
Capt. Smith
——— Tifdale
——— Rofs
Lieut. Daniel
———French
———Templeton
———Fitzgerald
———Sir Thomas Chapman
Cornet Cramer
———Gillefpie
———Longfield
———*Hon.* Geo. Pomroy
———Duncombe
Surgeon James Wallace

THE THIRD (OR PRINCE OF WALES'S) REGT. OF DRAG. GUARDS.

Major Gen. Phillipfon
Col. Manfell
Capt. Milbanke
——— Charlton
Lieut. Charlton
Cornet Dotten

TWENTIETH REGIMENT OF FOOT.

Colonel Lind
Major Hon S. D. Strangeways
———Rollinfon

C

SUBSCRIBERS.

Capt. Winchester
—— Norman
Lieut. Bateman
————Brooke
Ensign Wynyard

TWENTY-FIRST REGT. OF FOOT (OR R N B) FUZILEERS.

Colonel Hamilton
Major Lovell
Capt. Petrie
—— Brodie
Lieut. Grant
————Dalgleish
————Congalton
Qr. M. Geo. Lauder

TWENTY-FOURTH REGIMENT OF FOOT.

Lieut. Gen. Wm. Tayler
Lieut. Col. England
Major Pilmer
————Campbell
Capt. Blake
—— Stiel
—— W. Doyle
Lieut. Leybourne
————Short
————Hollings
Ensign Meyrick

General Trapaud, ——Berner's-Street
Col. Anstruther Thompson,—(late of 62 Regt.) Edinburgh
Samuel Toulmin, Esq.————Walbrook
Mr. James Turner, Jun.————Milbank
Thomas Trewin, Esq.————Helstone
John Trevener, Esq,————ditto
Mr. William Terwin,————Haymarket
Mr. Templeman,————Size-Lane
Edward Thornycroft, Esq.————Chester
Mr. William Truston,————Brentwood
Mr. John Thomas
Rev. Mr. Hen. Hawkins Tremayne, A.M. Heligan, Cornwall
Mr. Leigh Thorndon,
Thomas Fortune, Esq.————London

SUBSCRIBERS.

Mr. Thurgood,———Fenchurch Street
David Thomas, Esq.—Pay Master in America

U

The Rt. Hon.————The Earl of Upper Ossory
Mr. Benjamin Uphill,—Mount-Street, Grosvenor-Square
Cornelius Vanderstop, Esq.———Princes-St. Hanover-Sq.

W

The Rt. Hon.————The Earl of Westmoreland
The Rt. Hon.————The Earl of Winchelsea
The Rt. Hon.————The Earl of Waldegrave
The Rt. Hon.————The Earl of Warwick
The Rt. Hon.————Viscount Weymouth
The Rt. Hon.————Lord Willoughby de Broke
The Rt. Hon.———Lord Walpole
Sir Watkin Williams Wynne, Bart.—St. James's-Square
Sir George Warren, K B.———Grafton-Street
Miss Warburton
General Warde
Capt. Willoe,———(8 Regt. of Foot)
——— Wiseman,———(53 Regt. of Foot)
Edward Wilford, Esq.———Chelsea
——— Williamson, Esq.———Temple
Richard Whatley, Esq.————Parliament-Street
Rev. Mr. Whatley,————ditto
Rev. Mr. Wills,———Helstone
Mr. John Whitchead,———Basinghall-Street
Mr. Thomas Wagstaff,———Highgate
Mr. John Winpenny,———Bristol
Robert Woodriff, Esq.———Temple
Mr. Matthew White,———St. Swithin's-Lane
Woodmason and Page,———Leadenhall-Street
James Woodmason, Esq.———Bond-Street

Y

Major William Young

ERRATA.

VOL. I.

Page	Line	
15	12	after the word *to* add *them*
21	21	after *Frigate* add *who*
56	7 & 8	for *que d'arriver* read *qu'arriver*
60	—	Latin quotation misplaced, begin with the lower line
75	7	*seems to be* for *seem to be*
90	5	*Dura* for *duræ*
109	1 & 2	for *Enfant* read *Enfans*
124	19	for *and have* read *and they have*
141	10	for *petite* read *petit*
149	14	for *sont* read *font*
156	9	for *oculis* read *occultis*
195	10	for *stand as* read *stands a*
195	last line	after *celui* add *qui*
449	2	for *aud* read *should*

VOL. II.

Page	Line	
52	11	for *Fancis* read *Francis*
190	14	for 1788 read 1778
197	17	for *entertain* read *entertained*
221	last line	*esteeming* for *esteemed*
225	11	*were under* for *they were under*
283	16	for *making of Cyder* read *making Cyder*
288	15	omit the word *Old*
361	16	instead of *for* read *or*
376	2	omit *the* after *Year*
395	7	after *Purses* add *which*
425	18	*bearing* for *leaving*
480	6	after *be* add *had*
505	22	for *petits* read *petites*
506	1	for *true* read *trace*

TRAVELS

THROUGH THE

INTERIOR PARTS

OF

AMERICA.

LETTER I.

Cork, August 8th, 1776.

MY DEAR FRIEND,

I RECEIVED your letter, dated the 2d inftant, and furely nothing can be more flattering than the warm teftimony of regard and friendfhip every line of it fpeaks.—It was with great reluctance you confented to my going into the army, but a dull inactive life neither fuited my circumftances nor my inclination, and an early love

love of a military one, foon determined my choice. My time and poor abilities cannot be fo well employed, as in the fervice of my King and country.

I have no regrets at quitting England, but the lofs I muft fuftain in your pleafant and improving converfation; and am perfuaded you will alleviate as many of thofe painful reflections as poffible, by taking every opportunity of writing to me.— None fhall be omitted, on my part, of affuring you how often I think of you, and the implicit attention I fhall ever pay to your commands, in giving you a defcription of perfons, places, and various occurrences—and fhould I fometimes be too particular on trivial fubjects, you muft excufe it, and remember the two prevailing motives you affigned for this kind of correfpondence—the pleafure you was fo obliging to fay it would afford you, and the utility you thought it would be of to me,

by

by calling my attention to whatever became in the leaft worthy of obfervation.

This is the laft you muft expect from me on this fide the Atlantic, as in a few days we fail, with the care of fome recruits for the 47th regiment.

I once more entreat you, my dear friend, to take every opportunity of writing to me, and believe that time and diftance can never abate the refpect and friendfhip with which I am,

    Yours, &c.

LETTER II.

On board the Howe, on the Banks of Newfoundland. } Sept. 11th, 1776.

MY DEAR FRIEND,

IT would be very ungrateful indeed not to embrace the opportunity, by a ship that is bound for England, now lying too for letters, to send you a hasty account of the events that have happened since my departure from Ireland.

You know I had the care of some recruits for the 47th regiment; and as they were composed of that nation, no less famous for their characteristic errors, than their spirit and unbounded hospitality, let me relate a casual occurrence or two, in place of novelty, which cannot be expected, ed, fituated as I am, between fky and water.

There were continually fome little difputes among thefe Hibernians. One day, on hearing a more than ufual noife upon deck, I went up to enquire the occafion of it, and learnt it was a quarrel between two of them. Upon afking the caufe of him who appeared the tranfgreffor, he exclaimed, " Oh! and plaife your Honor, I " did nothing to him at all, at all"---when the other haftily replied, " Oh yes, and " plaife your Honor, he faid as how he " would take up a ftick and blow my " brains out." The peculiar manner in which it was vociferated, was fo truly comic, that I could not refrain from laughter, and merely reprimanding them, overlooked the offence.

The weather has been very pleafant, 'till a few days previous to our coming on these Banks, when there enfued a moſt dreadful ſtorm. The ſhip was unable to carry the leaſt ſail, being left to the fury of the driving tempeſt, it was impoſſible for any one to keep the deck, and the helm was laſhed hard of weather.

About the third day the ſtorm began to abate, and the evening became almoſt calm. But there was ſuch a prodigious ſwell of the ſea, that the ſhip was expected every moment to roll her maſts overboard: ſhe had driven ſo much to the leeward, that although we could not diſcern land, the yards and rigging were covered with birds, that were blown from it by the ſtorm.

At this time, one of my recruits coming upon deck, not obſerving any one there, and the ſea ſo tremendous, immediately went below, and cried out to his companions, " Oh! by my ſoul, honeys, the

" ſea

"fea is very dreadful, and we are all fure
"to be drowned, for the fhip's a finking.
"However, I have this confolation, that
"if fhe goes to the bottom, the Captain
"muft be accountable for us when we get
"to Quebec." And his fears operated fo powerfully, that he gave a groan, and fainted away.

A few days after this the fea, which before had been fo tremendous, and to ufe the technical phrafe, run mountains high, was now become as calm as a mill-pond. It is cuftomary, on fuch weather, in a fleet, for one fhip to invite the Captains and paflengers of others to dinner. The mode of invitation on thefe occafions, is by hoifting a table-cloth to the enfign-ftaff.

We hung out this fignal, and the Captain of the neareft fhip, with an officer, came on board. After dinner, fo fudden

and

and ftrong a breeze fprung up, as to render their return very unfafe, and it was two days before they could venture, when even then they accomplifhed it with imminent danger.

This is a little anecdote I cannot help wifhing to be much noticed, as it might be a caution to young officers and captains of fhips, how they make nautical vifits, or upon any occafion quit their veffels.

Thefe Banks may be ranked amongft the many furprifing and wonderful works of nature, being a mountain formed under water, by the flime that is continually wafhing away from the Continent. Its extent has never yet been afcertained, but is generally reckoned to be about 160 leagues long, and 90 broad. About the middle of it is a kind of bay, called the Ditch. The depth of water varies confiderably,

derably, being in some places only five, and in others sixty fathom. The sun is scarcely ever to be discerned, a cold thick fog generally covering the whole atmosphere, which renders it extremely dangerous to a fleet; for it is at times a state of total darkness, where a continual firing of guns, or incessant noise of the drum, can alone prevent the ships running foul of each other.

The winds around these Banks are generally very impetuous; the constant agitation of the waves, I am informed, is occasioned from the sea being driven by irregular currents, that beat sometimes on one side and sometimes on the other, striking with great force against the borders of these Banks, which are every where almost perpendicular, and repel them with equal violence: and yet, on the Banks themselves, a little from the coast, it is as quiet as in a bay,

bay, except there happens to be a ſtrong and forced wind coming from a great diſtance.

When we found we were upon theſe Banks, which is perceptible without founding, as the water changes from an azure blue to a white ſandy color, we laid too in order to fiſh for cod, the procefs of which is no lefs entertaining than ſurprizing to Europeans.

After baiting the hooks with the entrails of a fowl, in a few minutes we caught a fiſh, when the ſailors made uſe of ſome part of the entrails, as being a better bait, and then drew up the cod as faſt as you can poſſibly imagine; for though we remained there only half an hour, we caught as many as would ſerve the ſhip's crew the reſt of the voyage.

You may wonder by what means they are certain of having caught a fiſh, with

ſo

fo many fathom of line out. When it has been a little while in the water, they gently pull it with the finger and thumb, and if there is a fifh, the ftruggling of it occafions a vibration of the line, which is very perceptible, though fo many fathoms deep. They then haul it in, and as foon as the fifh comes in view, the water magnifies it to fuch a fize, that it appears almoft impoffible to get it on board; and indeed it requires fome dexterity, for on hauling them out of the water they ftruggle with fuch violence, as frequently to work themfelves off the hooks, by entangling the line in the rigging, before they can be got up the fhip's fide.

But thofe veffels which particularly follow this bufinefs, avoid the inconvenience by erecting galleries on the outfide, from the main-maft to the ftern, and fometimes the whole length of the fhip, in which are placed barrels with the tops ftruck out,

and

and the fishermen get into these to shelter themselves from the weather. Their stay, I imagine, cannot be long, as the method of curing is equally as expeditious as the catching them; for as soon as the cod is caught, they cut out its tongue, and give it to one who immediately strikes off its head, plucks out its liver and entrails, and giving it to another, the bone is drawn out as far as the navel; it is then thrown into the hold of the ship, where it is salted and ranged in piles. The person who salts it is careful to leave sufficient salt between the rows of fish, to prevent them touching each other, and yet not too much, as either excess would spoil the cod.

The right of fishing upon the Great Bank, by the law of nature, ought to have been common to all mankind; but England and France, being the only two powers that had colonies in North America, made no scruple to appropriate to themselves, what

what Spain certainly had the greateſt claim to, as the original diſcoverers of it; and who, from the number of her monks and prieſts, as well as her religion, might have pleaded the neceſſity of keeping. Yet at the concluſion of the laſt peace, they entirely gave up all pretenſions to it: ſince which time England and France are the only nations that frequent thoſe latitudes, and both have frigates continually cruizing, to prevent the encroachments of other nations.

The produce of this fiſhery is certainly a moſt inexhauſtible wealth to both countries, and it is no wonder they are ſo very tenacious of it: yet it is ſurprizing what a large circuit the ſhips are obliged to take before their voyage is compleated, and the profits reſulting from this fiſhery returns to either, nearly traverſing by water half the globe: for, in the firſt inſtance, they ſail from their reſpective ports

in

in Europe to thefe Banks, from whence they proceed with their cargoes to the Mediterranean and African iflands, where they difpofe of their fifh for the produce of thofe iflands, then go to the Weft Indies, to exchange that cargo, and return home laden with fugars and rum.

It appears a very fingular circumftance, that thefe Banks fhould abound with cod and no other fifh; and that the greateft philofophers have never been able to account for it.

The Captain of the fhip that is waiting for our letters growing impatient, obliges me to make a hafty conclufion, with wifhing you health and happinefs, and affuring you that you fhall hear from me as foon as I arrive at Quebec.

I am,
Yours, &c.

LETTER III.

Quebec, Oct. 8th, 1776.

DEAR SIR,

AFTER a fatiguing paſſage of eleven weeks, attended with no little danger, we are ſafe arrived at Quebec, which before I proceed to give you any deſcription of, it will be more methodical to relate the occurrences that befel us the remainder of our voyage.

I told you in my laſt, that we had frigates cruizing on the Banks, one of which informed us, that there were ſeveral privateers in the river Saint Laurence. Had we been leſs attentive to, and more apprehenſive of the ſhoals and ſands that river abounds with, rendering its navigation difficult

ficult and dangerous, it would have been better for us; for a few days after we had paſſed Cape Roſier, a favorable wind ſpringing up, the Captain crouded all the ſail he poſſibly could, in order to get the next morning to the iſle of Bec, where he might find a pilot, being very uneaſy, as he had never been up that river before.

But to our great ſurprize and aſtoniſhment, about one o'clock in the morning, we run right upon a ſhoal (which is called Mille Vache) with amazing violence.

A ſhip belonging to the fleet that had gone a head in the day time, and perceived the ſhoal, (being low water) had immediately brought too, to warn us of our danger, which they did, by firing ſignal guns. But the Captain miſtaking them for thoſe of a privateer, returned the ſhot.

The

The ship beat with great violence, and was every moment expected to go to pieces; but the tide soon turning, she rested upon the ground, and to our great astonishment, at the break of day, we found ourselves so near the shore, that, to use a sea phrase, we could almost chuck a biscuit on it.

Upon the clearing up of a fog, a ship was discerned, which proved to be the same that had fired guns in the night time: she was then about three leagues distant. We immediately fired guns of distress, of which she took no notice, and imagined she had, as too frequently is the case, deserted us, because we were in distress and stood in need of her assistance.

However, we found friends in a quarter we little expected, for a canoe with three men paddled from the shore, one of whom came on board and told us, we were very fortunate to have struck at the time of

Vol. I.   C   spring-

spring-tides, or there would be no probability of the ſhip's being got off. He directed us, when the tide was coming in, to carry out the bow anchor the length of the cable, and then made no doubt, but at the full, the ſhip would float again, and we might warp off.

After having given every proper inſtruction, he took his leave, requeſting, at the ſame time, that in caſe we were ſo unfortunate as not to effect it, we would come aſhore to his houſe, offering every aſſiſtance to ſave the cargo, and with a ſloop of his to take us up the river.

At the return of the tide ſome men were ſent out with the anchor, according to the directions given; at the heighth of it we floated, and to the joyful ſatisfaction of every one, got clear off, ſuſtaining no other damage than the loſs of two anchors: yet ſuch was the Captain's care and anxiety for
his

his owners, that, I am perſuaded, he would not have expreſſed half the concern for the loſs of the whole ſhip's burthen and company, that he did for his anchors: as with Captains of hired tranſports, the crew and the cargo are but ſecondary objects.

This is one inſtance of the numberleſs accidents that await tranſports, by which, I am convinced, the ſervice is retarded, and many operations, however critical, which depend on troops and proviſion, are often fruſtrated, either by deſign or negligence. For only figure to yourſelf what a ſituation an army of ſo many thouſands as that we have upon the Continent, and thoſe chiefly fed with proviſions from the Mother Country, muſt be in, upon the ſlighteſt delay.

It is much to be lamented, therefore, that all tranſports are not commanded by King's officers, or at leaſt the maſter made more subject to controul, when under convoy, or naval orders; as it would prevent the inconvenience and hazard that is continually happening to the King's service.

You will suppose it surprizing that this has never been noticed and remedied by those in power. I should have thought the affair of the powder-ship that went into Boston, would have occasioned a thorough investigation of this iniquitous business.

The Captains of transports in general, are a set of people who have their own interest much more at heart than the welfare of their country; and it is well known that many of them are disaffected to Government, which was the case of the Captain of the ship just alluded to, but where the blame is to be imputed, is not for me to say. As in all probability you may
not

not have heard of this affair, or the real truth of it may not have reached you, I fhall relate the matter, as I had it from a Captain of a fhip who failed in the fame fleet, whofe veracity can be relied on, and from the amazing ftrange circumftances which attended the lofs of that fhip, you may form your own opinions.

It feems this veffel was an immenfe charge, containing 1500 barrels of gunpowder, befides a great quantity of other warlike ftores. Several perfons well difpofed to Government, and who were perfectly aquainted with the Captain's principles, informed thofe who had the direction of tranfports at Cork, that this man would, the very firft opportunity, leave the convoy and join the Americans, but no attention was paid to the information; upon which they expreffed their apprehenfions to the Captain of the frigate was to convoy them out, who promifed to take all poffible care of that fhip during the voyage: and every one in the fleet thought he was not the man reprefented, as he kept clofe under the ftern of the frigate.

When the fleet came off Bofton harbour, a frigate that was cruizing for the purpofe, informed them, that the King's troops had evacuated Bofton, and gone to Halifax; and in the fleet's failing to that place, in one of thofe fogs that I have already defcribed to you, the Captain of the powder-fhip feized the opportunity, left the fleet, and failed back for Bofton, at the mouth of which harbour was ftationed a fifty-gun fhip, to prevent any veffel from going in, that might have efcaped any of the frigates that were cruizing.

Upon the Captain of the tranfport's being interrogated by the man of war, he acknowledged himfelf bound for Bofton,

ton, that he had not heard of the troops evacuating it, and several more excuses; but some doubts and suspicions arising from the man's converſation, and ſhe being found a ſhip of ſuch an immenſe treaſure, an officer was ſent on board her, and as the evening was coming on, laſhed her to his main-maſt, intending to ſail her the next morning for Halifax, under the beſt convoy he could afford.

But to ſhew you what a determined villain the Captain of the tranſport was, in the night time, he confined the Lieutenant, who was ſent on board, cut away from the man of war, and under cover of the night, made all poſſible expedition to get into Boſton.

The tide would not anſwer his purpoſe that time, and the man of war could not come up to her, for want of a ſufficient depth

depth of water. The Captain manned his pinnace, and sent another Lieutenant on board her. Upon the officer's attempting it, the Captain ſtruck a harpoon into his ſkull; he fell into the boat, and the reſt finding a great reſiſtance, and that they were likely to be overpowered, rowed back again.

The tide now turned, and he got the ſhip ſafe under the cannon of the Americans, before a greater force could be diſpatched to retake poſſeſſion of her.

The loſs on our ſide was great indeed, but the advantage to the Americans was tenfold, as they were in the utmoſt diſtreſs for thoſe materials, and which event may in ſome meaſure procraſtinate this unfortunate war.

Two days after our late accident, we arrived off the iſle of Condre, where we got a pilot, a pilot, and three days after anchored safe in the bason of this city.

Fearful of being too late to send this by a ship that is just sailing for England, there is only time to assure you, that I shall embrace every opportunity of convincing you, with how much sincerity and friendship I am,

Yours, &c.

LETTER IV.

Quebec, October 15th, 1776.

MY DEAR FRIEND,

BEFORE you have any account of this city and its environs, I shall describe to you the river Saint Laurence, which, upon their first sailing up it, is the astonishment and admiration of every European. In forming an idea of a river, people in general are apt to judge by comparison: those who have made the tour of Europe, instantly call to mind the Rhine and the Danube; those who have not, the Thames. What will you say, when you are informed that these, though very noble and beautiful, are but mere rivulets, when

put

put in competition with that of Saint Laurence.

This river iffues from lake Ontario, taking its courfe north-eaft, wafhing Montreal, where it receives the Outtuais, forming many fertile iflands, and a lake which is called St. Pierre. It continues the fame courfe, and meets the tide 400 miles from the fea, where it is navigable for large veffels. After receiving in its progrefs innumerable ftreams, this great river falls into the ocean at Cape Rofier; it is there 90 miles broad, where the cold in general is fevere, and the fea rather boifterous. In its progrefs it forms variety of bays, harbours and iflands, many of the latter being extremely fruitful and pleafant.

The river Saint Laurence has ever been looked upon as a good defence to this province, for in the neighbourhood of Quebec,

it

it abounds with hidden rocks, with ſtrong currents in many places, which force the ſhips to make various windings. From the time that Quebec was beſieged by Sir William Phipps, in the year 1690, who was obliged to retire with a great loſs of ſhipping, this river was very little known to the Engliſh till the year 1759, when Sir Charles Saunders, with a fleet of 50 Engliſh men of war, and near 300 ſail of tranſports, arrived off Quebec, without the loſs of a ſingle ſhip, which clearly proves thoſe dangers were not ſo great as had been repreſented. Since that time it has been better known; and though we have not at preſent at this place ſo many men of war, yet there are near as many tranſports, notwithſtanding the navigation up this river from the ſea is rendered very dangerous, by the ſtrength of the current and the number of ſand-banks, which frequently ariſe in places where they never appeared before; the fatal conſequences of

which

which feveral veffels have experienced this war.

There are abundance of porpoifes in the river St. Laurence, which are moftly white, and when they rife to the furface of the water, have the appearance of an hog fwimming. At night, if I may be allowed the expreffion, without being accufed of an Iricifm, they caufe moft beautiful *fire* works in the water: for being in fuch abundance, and darting with amazing velocity, a continued ftream of light glides through the water, and as fhoals of them frequently crofs each other, the luminous appearance is fo picturefque, that no defcription can reach it.

On our entering the river St. Laurence, we faw, off the ifland of Anticofti, a great number of feals, one of which we caught. This animal is generally ranked amongft the clafs of fifh, although produced on land,

land, and living more there than in water. Its head refembles that of a maftiff, it has four paws which are very fhort, efpecially the hinder ones, ferving rather to crawl, than to walk upon, and refembling fins; but the fore feet have claws; the fkin is exceeding hard and covered with fhort hair; they are firft white, but as they grow up turn to fandy or black, and fome of them are of three different colours.

There are two forts, the larger weighing near two thoufand pounds, and have a fharper fnout than the others. I have been told that the Indians have the art of taming thefe creatures, fo as to make them follow like a dog.

I am led to imagine they couple and bring forth their young on the rocks, from this reafon, wherein the powerful inftinct of nature fhewed itfelf very predominantly: one day, feveral large ones that had got
their

their young on their backs, dropt them now and then into the water and took them up again, which no doubt, as being brought forth upon land, was to teach them to fwim; it is not very furprizing, when it is confidered this animal is amphibious: but the mode is exactly the fame, only changing the element, with that of the feathered creation, whofe little ones flutter from fpray to fpray, before they venture to fly abroad. The eagle carries her young, to train them up to encounter boifterous winds.

Thefe animals are caught on the coaft of Labrador. The Canadians go to this frozen and almoft uninhabitable coaft, in the middle of October, and remain there till June; their mode of catching them is by placing nets between the continent and a few fmall iflands, where coming in fhoals from the eaft, in attempting to pafs thefe ftraights, they are caught; they then convey

vey them to land, where they remain frozen till the month of May; the oil is then extracted from them, and it is said that seven or eight of these animals will yield a hogshead. The use of its skin is so generally known, it needs no description; its flesh is allowed to be very good, but if you had partaken of it, as I have done, you would coincide with me in opinion, that it turns to better account when converted into blubber.

The tide goes a league beyond Trois Rivieres, which is thirty leagues higher up the river. The difference of the tide at this place is generally between forty-five and forty-eight feet, but at the new and full moon, from fifty-four to fifty-seven, which is very confiderable.

The river is three quarters of a mile broad here, and as the fea water, though it does not come up immediately to the town,

town, renders it fomewhat brackifh, the inhabitants make ufe of it only for culinary purpofes, having fpring water for their beverage.

In failing up the river St. Laurence, the firft plantations you meet with are about fifty leagues on the fouth, and twenty on the north fide of the river, below Quebec: they are but thinly fcattered, and their produce very indifferent. The fertile fields commence near the capital, which I am informed grow better, the nearer you advance to Montreal.

About half way up the river, we came to the *Ifles aux Oifeaux*, and paffed them about the diftance of a cannon fhot; they are two rocks that rife up in a conical form, about 60 feet above the furface of the water, the largeft of which appeared to be about two or three hundred feet in circumference; they are very near one another, and there does not appear a fufficient depth of water between them for a fmall fhallop. It is difficult to fay what color thefe are of, as both furface and banks are entirely covered with the dung of the birds that refort thither; however, there were difcernable in places fome veins of a reddifh caft.

One of the mates of the fhip faid he had been on them, and had loaded a fmall fhallop with eggs, which were of different forts, and that the ftench arifing from the dung was almoft infupportable. Befides the fea-gulls, and other fowls from the neighbouring lands, there is found a fpecies that cannot fly. It appears to me wonderful, in fo prodigious a multitude of nefts, how every one finds its own. At my requeft, the Captain of the fhip fired a cannon fhot, which fpread the alarm over all this feathered commonwealth, when there arofe over the two
iflands

islands a thick cloud of fowl, at least two or three leagues in circuit.

One material circumstance I forgot to mention to you, happened in our voyage to this place. In the middle of August, after we had been incommoded for several days with excessive heats, one morning, soon after we got up, we felt such an intense cold, that both the Captain and myself were obliged to put on our great coats. We could by no means imagine the cause of this alteration, the weather being extremely fine, and particularly as the wind did not blow from the north. But on the third morning, just before day-break, a sailor called out with all his might, " luff, luff," which the man at the helm had scarcely done, when an enormous piece of ice passed along-side of the vessel, which infallibly must have dashed her to pieces, had she struck against it. At day-break we saw it, when it appeared to be about six times as

large

large as our ship, and twice the heighth of its masts. You well know that only one third of ice, while swimming, appears above water, and when that is considered, I do not wonder that the ignorant should not readily assent to the relations given by travellers, of these frozen productions of nature.

Having already swelled this letter beyond its intended limits, and wishing to avoid, as much as possible, being too diffuse on trivial subjects, I shall conclude it with my best wishes for your welfare and happiness, assuring you that I am, with friendship and esteem,

Yours, &c.

LETTER V.

Quebec, Oct. 24th, 1776.

DEAR SIR,

AGREEABLE to my promife in a former letter, I fhall now proceed in the defcription of the river St. Laurence, with fome occurrences which befel us, previous to our arrival at Quebec.

One of the fineft bays to be met with in going up the river, is that of St. Paul, and as we were under the neceffity of anchoring oppofite to it, till the return of tide, I prevailed on the Captain to go on fhore.

Upon our landing, the Prieſt of the pariſh came and invited us to his houſe, treating us with much hoſpitality. He was a man rather advanced in years, a native of France, and poſſeſſed of great learning; he had been recommended by the French Court to the Biſhop of Quebec, while this province was under their government, and, as I am afraid is the caſe with too many well deſerving characters, was poorly rewarded, by being made Prieſt of this ſmall pariſh, for ſome eſſential ſervices he had rendered the French, which, however, has many privileges annexed to it.

From the great veneration and reſpect that was ſhewn him, one would naturally conclude he was much beloved by his pariſhioners, and his converſation turned upon making them happy, by inſtructing them both in religious and moral duties, encouraging induſtry, and diveſting them

of

of those innate savage dispositions, which, he observed, the lower sort of Canadians are but too prone to.

It was impossible to say which should be most admired, his smile of welcome, the neatness of the repast, or the hilarity of his conversation; all of which gave me the greater pleasure, when put in contrast with the other French Priests I have met with, who are austere and contracted, and so disgusting, that rather than sit down with them, I would eat hay with my horse.

This bay is about eighteen leagues below Quebec, containing only this small parish, which is some distance from the shore of the bay, on a low plain, formed by the river. It is surrounded with exceeding high mountains on every side, excepting one large gap, which runs parallel to the river. The farms are at some distance from each other, and the church is reckoned one of the moſt ancient in Canada, which ſeems confirmed by its bad architecture, and the want of ornaments; the walls are formed of pieces of timber, erected at two feet diſtance, which ſupport the roof, and between theſe timbers the ſpace is filled up with a kind of lime-ſlate. The church has no ſteeple, its roof is flat, and above this roof a bell is fixed in the open air. Moſt of the country around this bay belongs to the Prieſt, who lets it to the farmers.

The inhabitants chiefly live by agriculture, and the profits ariſing from their commerce in tar, which they extract from the red pine, by making an inciſion into the tree in the ſpring of the year, when the ſap is riſing, and before the tree has ſtopped running, it will produce ſeveral gallons of turpentine, which they eaſily manufacture into tar.

It

It may be conjectured, that the country situated upon the bay of this river being low, it was originally part of the bottom of the river, and was formed either by the decrease of water, or increase of earth, carried from the brooks, or thrown on it by storms, as a great part of the plants that grow here are marine. But in order fully to inform myself whether it was really as I apprehended, I enquired of several of the inhabitants, if ever they had found any shells in digging, who answered, that they had never met with any thing but different kinds of earth and sand.

There is one thing very remarkable, of which we had a proof: the wind is generally different in the bay to what it is in the river, for upon failing into the bay we had as favourable a wind as could blow, but in the moment of entrance, it was directly the reverse, which is thus acounted for: the bay being surrounded on all sides,
except

except one, with high mountains, and covered with tall woods, when the wind comes from the river, it ſtrikes againſt ſome of theſe mountains, where it is repelled, and conſequently takes an oppoſite direction.

The people who inhabit this bay, as likewiſe thoſe ſettled lower down the river, ſeem very poor; they have the neceſſaries of life in abundance, but debar themſelves of the comforts that ſhould ariſe from them, living chiefly upon bread and milk, and carrying their other proviſions, ſuch as butter, cheeſe, fleſh, poultry, eggs, &c. to market, where having diſpoſed of them, they purchaſe cloaths, brandy, and dreſſes for the women. Yet notwithſtanding their *pauvre* manner of living, they are always chearful and in high ſpirits.

Our object on going on ſhore was not ſo much to gratify our curioſity, as to procure

procure some vegetables; and as the Captain of the ship could not speak a word of French, as indifferent a Frenchman as you know me to be, I was obliged to be the interpreter on this occasion. I however made the inhabitants understand me very well, till I asked for some potatoes, by the usual school term of *pommes de terre*, and by which I understand they are called in France; yet, notwithstanding the Canadians are allowed to speak as pure French as at Paris, I could not make them comprehend what it was I wanted, the man continually saying, *Monsieur, je suis bien fâché de ne pouvoir comprendre ce que vous souhaitez*; at the same time expressing great uneasiness, as I repeatedly assured him, *que j'etois bien sur qu'il en avoit*, which seemed to vex him still more. However, in walking over his plantation, I happened to see a parcel in the corner of a shed; pointing to them I said, *Voila ce que je demande*, upon which, with great

great joy in his countenance, he exclaimed, *Oh! Monsieur, ce sont des putat, putat*; adding, with great heartiness, *Qu'il etoit bien aisé d'etre en etat de me satisfaire*. Upon my telling him, in England we called them *pommes de terre*, he added, with a remark which I should not have expected, *Que ce nom leur convenoit mieux que tout autre*. As I paid him very liberally for the vegetables we had of him, he said, with great expression of gratitude, *Ah! Monsieur, je me souviendrai toujours de vos bontés et des pommes de terre*.

Canada, from the fertility of its soil, and the salubrity of its climate, you would naturally imagine, contributed greatly to its own prosperity; but these, as in most other situations, are counterbalanced by its disadvantages. Canada has only one river for its exports and imports, and even this is so blocked up with ice, as not to be navigable

gable during fix months, while heavy fogs render the navigation flow and difficult the remainder of the year. And although the produce of Canada is fuperior to that of the other provinces, ftill the latter, not having fimilar impediments to encounter, will always have a decided advantage over this, in the convenience of almoft uninterrupted navigation.

The farm houfes are moftly built of timber, confifting of three or four rooms, and in one they have an iron ftove, which is rendered fo hot, as to communicate fufficient warmth to the reft. The roofs are covered with boards, and the crevices and chinks of the timbers are filled with clay, and their out buildings are thatched with ftraw.

Below the bay of Gafpey there is an ifland, called *Ifle Percée*; on your approach to it, it has the appearance of the fragment

ment of an old wall, being a fteep rock of about thirty fathoms in length, ten in heighth, and four in breadth, which the pilot told us was reported formerly to have joined *Mont Joli*, which ftands oppofite to it upon the Continent. This rock has in the center of it an opening, in the form of an arch (through which a fmall fchooner might pafs in full fail); from which circumftance, you will eafily imagine, it derives its name of *Ifle Percée*.

The laft object that attracts your attention before you enter the harbour of Quebec, is the ifle of Orleans, a moft beautiful large ifland, fituated in the middle of the river St. Laurence. It is feven leagues and a half long, and two broad, in the wideft part, very high, with fhores extremely fteep and woody, though in fome places there is a gradual defcent to the river, and where that is the cafe, it is entirely free from woods, and upon thefe

fpots

spots there are farm houses close to the shore.

The isle itself is well cultivated, and the eye is continually amused with large stone houses, corn fields, meadows, pastures and woods, with the addition of several good stone churches; some of which stand so close to the river, and it being Sunday when we passed the island, that we heard them at mass.

The river St. Laurence, till you come to this island, is mostly four or five leagues in breadth, but after you pass it, suddenly narrows, so as to be no more than a mile broad at Quebec, and from which circumstance this city derives its name, from the Indian word Quebeio, or Quebec, which signifies a strait or narrowing.

Shortly after we had passed this island, and turned Point Levy; we entered the harbour,

harbour, which has the appearance of a large bay, for Point Levy ſtretches itſelf out towards the Iſle of Orleans, ſo as to hide the ſouth channel; and that iſland projects ſo as to conceal the north.

On entrance, you are ſtruck with the grandeur and confuſion and variety of objects that preſent themſelves: fronting is the city; on the right is the beautiful fall of Montmorency, and a view up the river St. Charles; on the left there is an extenſive view up the river St. Laurence, and over the falls of Montmorency; a delightful proſpect of ſeveral leagues round the country, interſperſed with the villages of Beauport, Charlebourg, &c. a particular account of which I ſhall give you in my next.

I am, yours, &c.

LET-

LETTER VI.

Quebec, October 27th, 1776.

MY DEAR FRIEND,

IN my description of this province, you must not expect a tiresome detail of distances, or a romantic description of the country, but a few general observations, as I shall pass through the different parts of it, which are deserving notice.

This city, the capital of Canada, from the singularity of its situation, boasts of having that which no other city in the known world possesses, a fresh water harbour, an hundred and twenty leagues from

the fea, capable of containing an hundred
fhips of the line; it is built in the form of
an amphitheatre, on the declivity of a pe-
ninfula, formed by the rivers St. Laurence
and St. Charles, and commands a profpect
over extenfive fields, which appears rich,
lively and beautiful.

This city fuffered fo much during the
long fiege, laft winter, that it will by no
means anfwer the beautiful defcription
given by that elegant writer Mrs. Brookes,
in her Emily Montague, for many houfes
were deftroyed for fuel, others to prevent
harbouring the enemy, and fhot and fhells
continually defacing and burning the reft,
you muft eafily imagine, greatly contribute
to deftroy all ideas of regularity.

The city is divided into two towns, diftinguifhed by the *upper* and the *lower*,
which, during the fiege, were feparated by a
ftrong

ſtrong ſtockade, which proved extremely fortunate for us, as the enemy got into the lower town, but not being able to keep poſſeſſion, they ſet it on fire, and nearly deſtroyed the whole of it.

There are two communications from the lower to the upper town, the one for carriages, by a ſerpentine road up a very ſteep aſcent, and the other for foot paſſengers, up a flight of ſteps cut out of the rock.

The carriage road to the upper town, as well as the ſtreets in general, are almoſt impaſſable for either man or beaſt, never having been paved ſince the ſiege, when the pavement was entirely torn up, that the ſhells might bury themſelves in the ground before they burſt, whereby they were rendered leſs dangerous.

The diſtreſſes of the inhabitants in a beſieged town, at all times are very great; but

but here they were rendered particularly fo, from the extreme feverity of the weather, being deprived of fuel, and compelled to refide in their cellars, as the only place that could afford them the leaft fhelter.

The Governor's houfe ftands upon an high eminence, and being bomb-proof, the family thought themfelves in perfect fecurity: from its elevation too, it was imagined to be out of the reach of cannon fhot. One evening, however, they were rather unpleafantly convinced of their error, by a fhot paffing through an adjoining room to that in which they were playing at cards; this threw them into no little confufion, and obliged them to retire to that part of the houfe in which the other inhabitants were compelled to refide.

You may remember, fome months before my departure from England, that Mr.

Mr. W---, who is a *bon vivant*, jocularly remarked, if he were confined to any single room, it should be the cellar; he was then at the Governor's, enjoying his favourite wish, happy as good company and good wine could make him, the sound of every cannon being the signal for a bumper.

A Major who was here during the siege, expressed his astonishment to me that the place held out so long, having an amazing severity of weather, and numberless other difficulties to encounter; and that its safety was entirely owing to the great exertions of General Carleton, who continually encouraged the inhabitants to action, for they chiefly composed the strength of the garrison.

The suburb of *St. Fauxbourg* is entirely destroyed, but that, as well as the lower town, is now rebuilding, and when compleated, must add greatly to the beauty of the city. There are several quays, and a convenient place for heaving down ships to be repaired, called *Cul de Sac*, where the King's ships lay up during the winter, to preserve them from danger upon the freezing and breaking up of the ice, which is more hazardous than you can imagine; for unless the ships are got into this *Cul de Sac* in proper time, they are very much damaged, and sometimes totally lost, by the amazing islands of ice that float down the river.

This city is at present badly accommodated as to taverns, there being but one in the upper, and another in the lower town, both of them in the worst state imaginable; for although they provide good dinners, the rest of the accommodations are such as would disgrace the meanest public-house in London. No attendance whatever from servants; no seperate apartments, and fifteen or twenty people are obliged to

sleep

sleep in one room, about a yard apart from each other; usually deprived of natural rest in such vile dormitories, one scarcely feels refreshed the whole day, and let me assure you, since I have been here, I have not enjoyed a good night's repose, from the sonorous music I am surrounded with, arising from that natural and almost universal wind instrument, the nose. The owners of these taverns imagine, if they give good dinners and good wine, they perform wonders. This, however, may be said in their favour, as to accommodation, that this city has been for many months past in a very deranged state, owing to the late siege.

The Canadians of the higher class are very polite and attentive to strangers; a few days since, I was invited to dine with one of the principal merchants, *chez Monsieur Roberdeau*; the dinner was entirely after the French fashion, and displayed with much taste, but such was the perverseness of my English stomach, that it could not relish one of their made dishes; and although I endeavoured to eat, out of compliment, the master of the house perceived I did not do it with any gusto; he then said, *Ah! Monsieur, vous ne faites que d'arriver dans ce pays; quand vous aurez été avec nous un certain tems, vous aimerez beaucoup notre cuisine. Je suis bien fâché que dans ce moment il ne se trouve rien à votre gout, mais quand vous me ferez l'honneur de venir une autrefois chez moi, j'aurai soin d'avoir du* ROAST BEEF *et du* PLUMB PUDDING *que les Anglois aiment tant.* When the desert came, which was before the cloth was removed, I made amends for my not being able to eat at dinner, which the master of the house observing, said, *Ah! Monsieur, ce n'est pas que vous ne vous souciez pas des viandes, mais c'est que vous etes un peu comme les enfans, vous aimez les friandises;* when, fearful lest I should be displeased at his raillery, with

a polite-a politeness truly French, he filled his glass, and added, *Allons, Monsieur, versez et vive le Roi d'Angleterre.*

Fearful of losing the opportunity that now presents itself of conveying this to England, I have but just time subscribe myself,

Yours, &c.

LET-

LETTER VII.

Quebec, October 30th, 1776.

MY DEAR FRIEND,

THE hasty conclusion I was obliged to put to my last, having prevented me from entering so fully into the description of this city as I had intended, I now transmit to you some further particulars relative to its siege, and the religion of its inhabitants.

The causeway by which General Montgomery made his attack, is not more than twenty-four feet wide; on one side is a lofty perpendicular rock, and on the other a steep precipice, without any fence, down

to

to the river; this causeway was defended by two strong barriers, and were I induced to give an opinion, nothing but a desperate effort could justify the attack. The event fatally proved it; for upon the advance of the enemy, the first barrier was abandoned, which, after they had broke down, flushed with success; and the hopes of easily gaining the upper town, they rushed on (with an intrepidity that might expect every thing from their valor) to the second barrier, where two pieces of cannon were concealed, and upon their approach were immediately fired, when great numbers of them were killed and wounded, and in their retreat many fell down the precipice; this defeat greatly contributed to put an end to the siege, the termination of which, had nearly been frustrated, by the eager impetuosity of the sailors, who were posted with those guns, as they could scarcely be restrained from firing them when the enemy attacked the

first

first barrier, which, if they had done, the slaughter would not have been so great, nor the enemy perhaps have lost their brave Commander. But by the threats of the officers upon duty at that post, the guns were not fired till the enemy were within a few yards of them; and as they advanced abreast, as many as the causeway would admit of, you may easily conceive what havoc there must have been amongst them.

In this daring enterprize fell a man, who lived long enough to establish a reputation, *Nec poterit ferrum, nec edax abolere vetustas, quod nec Jovis ira nec ignis,* as no doubt it will be handed down by the Americans to the latest ages. He died too soon for the support of that unnatural faction, to which, from mistaken principles, he was deeply attached; and being a man worthy of some notice, you shall know the little history I have been able to collect of him.

In

In the laſt war he was an officer in our ſervice, and diſtinguiſhed himſelf in ſeveral inſtances. At the peace he came over to this country, and married an American lady, where by his conduct and agreeable manners, he was reſpected as much as if he had been a native; and being, from his marriage and long reſidence in the country, conſidered as a man fit to be truſted with a command, he was appointed Brigadier General by the Congreſs; this commiſſion he wiſhed to decline, feeling a compunction, as a native of Great Britain, and once in the King's ſervice, to bear arms againſt his Sovereign. His wavering inclination was unfortunately ſubdued, by the over-perſuaſion of a fond wife, whom he loved moſt affectionately, and the importunate ſolicitation of his relations and friends. When he had taken a decided part, his conduct fully correſponded with the high opinion that had been formed of his abilities and fidelity. No one who lived ſo

ſhort

short a time in their employ, could render them more important services, or do their cause more honor.

When he had been induced to sacrifice the happiness he enjoyed in private life, and enter into the service of the Congress, he was then absolved from all views adverse to their party (of which he had been suspected) and considered as a man who took a part in the cause from conscience and principle. In this light he was viewed while living, and spoken of when dead. He had the singular felicity of being equally esteemed by the friends and foes of the party he espoused; the latter acknowledged his worth, though they reprobated the cause in which he fell. To the praise of General Carleton, his remains were, by the General's order, interred with all military honors.

An

Very shortly after this repulse, an American soldier, in attempting to step out of his *batteaux*, at Wolfe's Cove, fell into the water, and catching hold of a flake of ice that was floating down the river, he got upon it, and was carried down the stream. As he passed Quebec close to the shore, he was seen by a centinel, who observing a man in diftrefs, called out for help, when numbers flew to his affiftance, and found him motionlefs; by the help of fpirituous liquors, with fome difficulty they brought him to life for a moment, and juft recovering fpeech enough to tell them, that the city would not long be in our poffeffion, he inftantly expired.

A mile from the city is a Convent, that was once poffeffed of a beautiful garden, but this, as well as their chapel, with the images and other ornaments of their religion, are greatly injured. The enemy,
after

after taking poffeffion of the Convent, converted it into an hofpital, and compelled the nuns to attend upon their fick and wounded; and what was ftill more perfecuting to their religion than to their wifhes, feveral of the nuns, after they had abandoned it, proved capable of in fome meafure making up for the ravages of war, by producing what may in future become the ftrength and fupport of their country.

There are feveral churches in each town, but thofe in the upper are the moft magnificent, and have fuftained the leaft damage. The largeft of thefe churches, and what may be termed the cathedral, has nothing worthy of notice, except a handfome fteeple; it is entirely roofed with flate, and is the only building I obferved that has this advantage, they being all covered with fhingles. It is much ornamented in the infide; the gallery is bold,

light,

light, and well wrought, furrounded with an iron balluftrade, painted and gilt, of curious workmanfhip; one thing, however, appears very fingular, that the pulpit is likewife gilt, and feems to have had more labor beftowed *upon*, than it is ever likely to have *within* it; there are three altars handfomely defigned, and fome good pictures; it is without any dome or cupola, having only a flat ceiling, very curioufly ornamented; it is not as in moft Cathedrals, paved with ftone, but floored with planks, which makes this church the more fupportable in winter; in others you are generally ftarved to death with cold. After the Romifh fervice is over, on a Sunday, the Governor, with the officers and foldiers of the garrifon, and the Proteftant inhabitants of the city, refort thither to their worfhip. This little circumftance I mention to you, as the paffing of the Quebec bill made fuch a noife in England; clearly to fhew there is no animofity among the inhabitants, on the fcore of religion. Where the Canadians, who conftitute the principal part of the inhabitants of this province, did not interfere with our religion, I cannot but think it was a very neceffary and politic ftep in Government to tolerate theirs; as at the time the bill paffed, it was judged proper to make this facrifice to them, in order to gain their affections, which feemed to be wavering, whether they fhould not join the other provinces in rebellion againft England.

For my own part, I am led to imagine, from the converfation I have had with feveral of the principal inhabitants, they never were in the leaft apprehenfive of their religion being fuppreffed, but that idea was inftilled into their minds by fome party at home, who, I am forry to obferve, are more dangerous than any enemy we can poffibly have abroad.

With

With all the advantages of the laws of our conftitution, the toleration of their religion, and the bleffings of liberty, the Canadians are by no means well affected to the Englifh Government, but have a ftrong propenfity to be under the protection of the French; and, I am confident, would affift the Americans, had we not fuch a powerful force in this province.

The garrifon of this city, and a few inhabitants at Montreal, are ftaunch to the interefts of Government; for their fidelity and courage have been proved; upon the commencement of the fiege, the General ordered every one out of the city, that he could entertain the leaft fufpicion of, none of whom have fince made their appearance.

The army is now returning from the Lakes, and at prefent the garrifon confifts of Colonel Maclean's regiment, and the

recruits

recruits lately arrived from England; the 34th regiment is daily expected, as the army is getting into winter quarters. General Carleton and General Burgoyne are both here, the latter of whom fails for England in a few days.

My friend Captain W---n, who is embarking for that country where my fondeft wifhes are placed, will deliver you this: he has juft called upon me for my letters. I muft therefore conclude. You fhall hear from me by the lateft fhip that fails.

Yours, &c.

LETTER VIII.

Quebec, Nov: 4th, 1776.

MY DEAR FRIEND,

VISITING two or three of the villages round this city, has enabled me to give you some little description of the country and its inhabitants.

About Charlebourg and Beauport it is rather *champaign*, but becomes more woody towards Lorette. The farm houses interspersed about the country are very numerous, and being generally whitened on the outside, form a neat and picturesque appearance: their houses mostly consist of one floor, very few having a story to them, which gives rise to the idea, that the Canadians

nadians will *tell* a ftory well, though they never *make* one.

You would be pleafed to find them extremely neat in their houfes, very attentive to their cattle, and careful of the ftock on their farms. They are at prefent employed in cutting and getting in wood for the winter, for themfelves and the market, for though it is fo early, there has been a fevere fall of fnow; wood-cutting continues all this month, and in December, when the winter is fet in, it is carried into the city upon fleighs over the fnow, being a much eafier conveyance than with carts, as the roads are fo intolerably bad.

The Canadians in general are a fwarthy people, and low in ftature; their drefs confifts of a kind of jacket, and when the weather is cold, a blanket coat, which they faften round them with a worfted fafh. They moftly wear a woollen cap,

but

but in the cold weather a fur one, and have amazing long queues, of which they are exceedingly proud. They are seldom or ever found without a pipe in their mouths, a habit which they acquire in their very infancy. I was much surprized upon going into one of their houses, in which there was a large family, mostly boys, to find, that from the youngest up to the father, they all smoaked; nay, one of three years old had a pipe in his mouth. Their usual mode of living being chiefly milk and vegetables, which, joined to the number of the fast days imposed on them by their religion, renders them a very meagre and slender people.

The women are extremely lively, good-natured and obliging, and very neat in their persons, but have not the least pretension to beauty. The men are far from agreeable, for since they have enjoyed the blessings of an English Government, they are become infolent and overbearing, eafily offended, and when they fancy themfelves fo, their cry is, *Je vais le dire au General Carleton*; and the General is of that good-natured, affable difpofition, that he always liftens to their complaints, and is continually plagued and tormented with fome of the moft trivial nature, by thefe troublefome and tenacious people, for they conceive their Governor is bound to hear them, efpecially their *Seigneurs*, or Lords of the village; it is a title you have not among you, but I affure you thofe who poffefs it here, fancy themfelves of no little importance, and affume more confequence than the firft peer in England.

Thefe *Seigneurs* are defcendants of thofe officers and gentlemen who firft fettled, and had grants in this province, when Canada was only a vaft foreft; who, not being proper perfons to cultivate it themfelves, nor poffeffed of a fufficient fund to pay labourers,

ers, let out the grounds at a very slender quit rent; so that with the fines, which were here very small, and what is called the *Droit du Moulin, & Metairie,* a lordship, which consists of two leagues in front, and an unlimited depth, can yield them no great revenue; and there are many planters on their manors, who by their industry have become wealthier than the owner himself; notwithstanding which they stand in great awe of these *Seigneurs,* as they are descended from antient nobility in France, the forefathers of whom were permitted by Louis XIV. to exercise commerce as well by sea as land, without question, interruption, or derogating from their quality and rights; and to you, who so well know the French, I need not say in what manner any one descended from nobility conducts himself, and the *hauteur* he treats every one with.

About

About three leagues from this city is a nation of Indians, who live at a small village called Indian Lorette: they are quite civilized, have a church, go regularly to mass, and are extremely ingenious in making bead ornaments.

These Indians, who are really Christians, of the Romish persuasion, have a chapel built nearly on the model, and of the same dimensions as that I have heard you relate you met with in Italy, of *Santa Casa*, and, as in that, have an image of the Virgin, which, upon enquiry, appears to be a copy of that very statue. Whether it was the effect of imagination, devotion, or of any other cause, I cannot say, but upon attending the chapel, I was seized with an inward and sacred terror, of which I can give no account. The solid piety of the Indians, (whom we are taught to believe so naturally ferocious, as no edification, religious or moral, can overcome)

added,

added to the gloomy horror of the situation, made a violent impreffion upon me, which became the more ftrong, upon obferving the fervor and modefty which they difplayed in their devotions.

Thefe Indians had a great number of dogs with them, which feems to be the only domeftic animal they breed; they are trained up for hunting, and are equal to any hounds; appearing to be all of one fpecies, having upright ears, of dark brindled color, with a long fnout, like that of a wolf. None of our Englifh dogs are more remarkable for their fidelity, which is rather to be wondered at, being but very ill fed, and never careffed by them.

As hereafter, and no doubt before my return to England, I fhall meet with many Indians of different nations, cuftoms and manners,

manners, give me leave to make a few reflections upon thefe favages, as they are called, and civilized man.

In regard to the former, their origin and antiquity is quite uncertain; the only matter, therefore, to be confidered is, whether thefe untutored nations are more or lefs happy than us? Whether they, who are in the condition of man left to mere animal inftinct, paffing their lives in hunting, feeding, producing their fpecies, and repofing themfelves, do not pafs a life of more felicity than ours, who can enjoy every luxury of life, and vary our indulgences and wants in a thoufand ways?

It is in our nature and difpofitions, that we muft look for the means of happinefs. Wherein then does it confift? Prefent fubfiftence, and (which I think there can be none fo hardened as not to have) a thought of futurity, and the hopes of enjoying

every

blessing that is attendant on it. The savage never is in want; he lays in no stores, because the earth and waters are reservoirs to supply them. Fish and game are to be had all the year. The savage has no house to secure him from the inclemency of the external air, or commodious fire places, his furs answering all these purposes. His labor is but for his own benefit; he sleeps when he is weary, and is a stranger to restless nights. Little does he experience weariness that arises from unsatisfied desires, or that uneasiness of mind which springs from prejudice or vanity. As far as I can perceive, the Indian is subject to no evils but those inflicted by nature.

In what manner then do we enjoy a greater happiness? Our food may be more wholesome and delicate, our cloaths may be softer, and our habitations secure us better against the weather; but then observe the common people, who are the support

port of civil fociety; the number of men who in all ftates bear the burthen of labor; can they be faid to be happy, who, by the luxury and police of their governments, are reduced to a ftate of fervitude? And to what outrages are thofe in a higher fphere expofed to? If you are poffeffed of any property, you know not how far it may be called your own, but muft, in all probability, divide the produce between the lawyer, in teaching you how to preferve it, and the collector, who comes to levy unlimited taxes. If you have no property, how can you be affured of a permanent fubfiftence? What induftry or invention is fecure againft the viciffitudes of fortune, or the encroachment of others.

In the forefts of America, if there is any fcarcity in the north, the favages bend their courfe to the fouth; but in our civilized ftates, we are confined within certain limits, where if famine, or war, or peftilence,

with

with all their concomitant horrors, fhould befal us, all muft participate.

It certainly is apparent to every one, that injuftice prevails in the partial diftribution of fortunes and ftations, which muft be the effect and the caufe of oppreffion. In vain does cuftom, prejudice, ignorance, or hard labor, ftupify thofe of the lower clafs, fo as to render them infenfible of their degradation; it is not in the power of religion or morality to hinder them from feeing and feeling the arrangements of policy, in the diftribution of what we call good and evil; and, no doubt, you muft have often heard a poor man expoftulating with heaven, " What have I done, that I fhould deferve to be born in fuch an indigent and dependent fituation ?"

The reafon we prefer our condition to that of the favages is, becaufe civilization has

has rendered us incapable of bearing some natural hardships, which they can endure; and simply that we are attached to some indulgence custom has made necessary to us. As a proof of this assertion, and how a civilized man may habituate himself to the society of savages, and return to this state of nature, let me relate the situation of a Scotchman, who was cast away upon the Island of *Fernandez*, where he lived alone; his only enjoyments consisted in supplying his wants, and to such a pitch had his ideas of happiness raised themselves, that he forgot his country, his language, his name, and even the articulation of words. And after a banishment of four years, from the burthens of social life, he had lost all thought of the past, or anxiety for the future.

One of the first principles we imbibe, one of the first instincts of man, is a consciousness of independence; and no doubt

doubt but you muſt have obſerved, that the man who poſſeſſes a competent ſubſiſtence is incomparably happier than the rich man, who is reſtrained by prejudices and faſhions, which inceſſantly are reminding him of the loſs of his liberty, and which too frequently are the occaſion of the raſh and fatal act of ſuicide.

In comparing the ſtate of the ſavages to that of children, the queſtion may eaſily be decided, which has been ſo warmly in debate among the moſt learned men, "whether the ſtate of nature has the advantage over that of ſocial life?" And you, no doubt, will readily allow, that your ſtate of childhood, notwithſtanding the reſtraint of education, was the happieſt period of your life. Nothing ſurely can more clearly indicate the happineſs that children feel, than that habitual chearfulneſs they demonſtrate, when not under the ſchoolmaſter's rod.

After all, a single word may determine this great question. Let us ask the civilized man if he is happy; and the savage whether he is unhappy? If they both answer in the negative, there is an end of the dispute.

How mortifying must this parallel be to civilized nations? And the more painful the reflection, as it awakens the feelings to the cause of their sufferings; no doubt but they will one time or other be convinced from whence it arises---from the confusion of their opinions, from the defects of their political constitutions, and from the capriciousness of their laws, which ever are in continual opposition to the laws of nature. But for fear you think I am growing too sententious, I shall return to my description of this province.

The woods of Canada abound with a large kind of rabbits, which are of a brown color in the fummer, and turn white in the winter, one of the effects of the extreme cold or fnow that prevails in this climate; we found likewife vaft quantities of partridges, much larger than ours, which the Canadians call pheafants; there are two forts of them, the fpruce and the pine: the meat of the former is very delicious, to thofe who are fond of the flavor of the fpruce. The market at this place is well fupplied with all kind of provifion, fifh and vegetables in abundance.

The place beft adapted to repay the labours of the hufbandman, are pointed out to him by the fpontaneous productions of nature; where the pine, the fir-tree, and the cedar grow folitarily, there he finds only watry and fandy grounds: but wherever the foil is covered with maple, oak, beech, yoke, elm, hickory, and fmall cherry-

cherry-trees, there he is certain to meet with a reward for his trouble of clearing away the woods, and may expect a great increafe, without the difficulty of manuring.

Being informed that the pacquet fails this afternoon, and having feveral other letters to write, a further account of this province muft be delayed till my next; and in hopes you will pardon my breaking off fo abruptly, and leaving you in a ftate of fufpence, I remain,

Yours, &c.

LETTER IX.

Quebec, November 5th, 1776.

MY DEAR FRIEND,

OBLIGED to conclude my laſt rather haſtily, I ſhall reſume my obſervations on this province, without any apology.

Moſt of the plantations in Canada are ſufficient to ſupply the wants of their reſpective owners, and there are few of them that do not yield rye, maize, barley, flax, hemp, tobacco, pulſe and pot-herbs, in great abundance, and thoſe of an excellent quality.

It is capable of furnifhing many articles for a trade with the Weft Indies, which was wholly neglected, whilft this province was under the French Government; but fince in our poffeffion, great quantities of flour, planks, and timber, proper for building, have been exported to them: and as there is perhaps no country in the whole world which produces more forts of wood, or of a better quality, you may eafily judge what immenfe riches may be drawn from thence, it confifting principally of woods.

I know not whether giving you an account of the extenfive forefts of Canada, will afford you any entertainment; but when I inform you that they have the appearance of being as ancient as the world itfelf, and were never planted by the hand of man, I think you will find fome amufement in the defcription of them.

On my firſt arrival in this country, I was ſtruck with the loftineſs of the pines, fir-trees, and cedars, which are of a ſize perfectly aſtoniſhing. There are two ſorts of pine, both of them yielding turpentine. The white pines produce, on their upper extremities a kind of muſhroom, which the Canadians adminiſter in caſes of the dyſentery. The red pines contain more turpentine, are heavier, and do not grow to ſuch a thickneſs; but where they flouriſh, the land is reckoned very good to raiſe corn.

There are ſeveral ſpecies of fir-trees, which riſe to a great height, are excellently calculated for maſts, as well as every ſort of carpenter's work.

There are two ſorts of cedars too, the white and red, the former of which grows the thickeſt, and the odour is in its leaves; whereas, in the latter, the odour is in the wood,

wood, and far more agreeable. Of thefe trees the Canadians make palings, but moftly fhingles for covering their houfes, from its extreme lightnefs.

All over Canada are two forts of oak; the white grows in low fwampy grounds, the red in dry fandy lands.

There are three forts of walnuts; the hard, the foft, and another with a thin bark. The hard fort bear a fmall nut, very good to eat, but apt to occafion coftivenefs, the wood of which is only fit to burn. The tender bears a large fruit, with a hard fhell, the kernels of which are excellent: the wood of this tree is fingularly curious, being almoft incorruptible in water or in the ground, and difficult to confume in the fire: of this wood the Canadians make their coffins. The third fort produces a nut which is exceedingly bitter, but

but yields an excellent oil, ufed by the inhabitants for their lamps,

Beech and elm trees are in great abundance; and in the thickeft woods are found vaft numbers of cherry and plumb-trees.

There are an infinite number of others, but as I am no Botanift, you will pardon my giving an account of what is here in fuch variety, that perfons who have taken the moft unremitting pains to difcover them, have not been capable of defcribing half their number, I fhall conclude this heavy detail of trees, with that of the maple, which boafts of many excellent qualities.

The maple tree yields in great quantities a liquor which is cool and refrefhing, with an agreeable flavor. The Canadians make a fugar of it, a very good pectoral, and ufed for coughs. There are many
trees

trees that yield a liquor they can convert into fugar, but none in fuch abundance as the maple. You will no doubt be furprized to find, in Canada, what Virgil predicted of the Golden Age, *Et dura quercus fudabunt rofcida mella.*

The ftock of the farming part of the inhabitants in this province, confifts generally of about a fcore or two of fheep, ten or twelve cows, and five or fix oxen for the plough; the cattle are fmall but excellent, and the people, fince they have been under the Englifh Government, live in a degree of eafe and happinefs unknown to the country people in England, and are now improving their farms and enriching themfelves very faft. Before the commencement of the war, they ufed to export vaft quantities of wheat and all forts of grain, to the other provinces and the Weft India iflands; but when under the French Government, they were fo oppreffed by their

Seigneurs,

Seigneurs, that they never raised more grain than would serve themselves and the stock on their farms; whenever they did, it was generally claimed by the *Seigneurs* for the use of Government. The Canadians were at that time a very indolent set of people: now they reap the sweets of their industry, and are quite the reverse.

I went yesterday to view the Fall of Montmorency, which is really beautiful. The breadth of it is not above ten or twelve yards, and its perpendicular height one hundred and twenty feet; by the violent fall of such an immense body of water, there is always a thick fog of vapors, which occasions a continual rain, for some distance round the bottom. Anxious to examine it as minutely as possible, I approached within twelve yards of the Fall, when a sudden gust of wind blew such a thick fog off the spray, that in less than a minute I was as wet as if I had walked half

an

an hour in a heavy fhower, which, however, did not prevent my endeavouring to fatisfy my curiofity, for I perfevered, in hopes of accomplifhing my wifh, which, like many of our ardent purfuits, did not bring me that recompence I had flattered myfelf it would; for having obtained the purport of my intention, inftead of the beautiful appearance I had pictured to my imagination, to be difcerned between the rock and the immenfe body of water that was falling from fuch a prodigious height, I found myfelf enveloped in a very thick fog of fpray, fcarcely able to fee my hand when extended, and where, in all probability, if I had continued five minutes, and the wind changed, I was in danger of being drowned. The noife occafioned by the fall was fo great, that an officer who was with me was obliged to fpeak as loud as he could, to make me underftand any thing he faid. It is fometimes heard at Quebec, which is two leagues diftant to the fouthward, and
when

when that is the cafe, it is the fign of an approaching ftrong north-eaft wind.

One thing remarkable is, that this plentiful fall of water, which never dries up, one would imagine, muft proceed from fome fine river: but it is quite the reverfe, it being only a puny ftream, which in fome places is fcarcely fufficient to cover the ankle; it flows, however, conftantly, and derives its fource from a pleafant lake, twelve leagues diftant from the falls.

I have vifited the plains of Abraham, to fee the remains of the enemy's encampment, and could not help contrafting thofe who had fo lately abandoned that place, with the poffeffors of it when the brave Wolfe fell! Nor was it poffible to fupprefs a figh to the memory of that gallant officer, who, at fo early a period in life, had acquired the efteem and admiration of all mankind. While in the very arms of death,

he

added glory and conqueſt to the Britiſh empire.

Nor could I help lamenting, at the ſame time, the fate of an officer of conſiderable merit, though an enemy, the brave Montgomery, who commanded the troops that had ſo lately abandoned this encampment, and of whom I have already ſpoken: he poſſeſſed all the fire of military ardor, ruſhed with impatience in the front of every danger, and met his death, " e'en at the cannon's mouth," where he unfortunately fell a ſacrifice to miſtaken principles, unnatural rebellion, and the ambitious views of a few deſigning men.----His courage and death would have done honor to a better cauſe.

The people in this city are making preperations for the winter, and you would think it impoſſible they could conſume the amazing rafts of timber that are already floated

floated down the river; but I am informed they are a very inconfiderable part of what are expected.---It is not in the leaft furprizing they were obliged to pull down houfes for fuel laft winter, during the fiege.

Europeans muft form a terrible idea of the intenfe cold of this country, from the preparations the Canadians take to guard againft it; for the inhabitants are pafting paper round their windows, and every crevice where they imagine the leaft cold will penetrate.

Inftead of fire-places they make ufe of iron ftoves, which muft be extremely unhealthy; a few days fince I went into a room when there was a fire in one of them, and had not been there above five minutes, when I was feized with a moft intolerable head-ach, which I can only attribute to the fulphureous air that proceeds

ceeds from thefe ftoves; and, for my own part, imagine they are the occafion of the Canadians having fuch fallow complexions; but cuftom, which in fome meafure overcomes all prejudices, will no doubt reconcile me to them.

The fhips are all preparing to fail for England, left the river fhould freeze up.

I have been this afternoon upon the ramparts, to fee the Apollo frigate drop down, in which General Burgoyne fails for England; who, I am perfuaded, has the fincere and ardent wifhes of all ranks in the army, for his fafety and happy arrival. The General joins to the dignity of office, and ftrict attention to military difcipline, that confideration, humanity, and mildnefs of manners, which muft ever endear him to all who have the happinefs to be under his command; for my own part, I fhall pray with Shakefpear, " that the

the winds of all the corners may kifs the fails, and make his veffel profperous."

I remained on the ramparts to take the laft look of the Apollo, who, with a fteady and favourable breeze, failed magnificently down the river, and was foon out of fight. You cannot guefs how it affected me; fhall I confefs that more than once I wifhed myfelf on board her: it was fuch a fight as muft awaken the mind to all its natural attachments. But that I may not think too much of country and friends, at this time, I fhall haftily conclude myfelf,

Yours, &c.

LETTER X.

Montreal, November 16*th*, 1776.

MY DEAR FRIEND,

AFTER a tedious march of near three weeks, which for a young foldier is a pretty good initiation into the toils of his profeffion, I am fafe arrived at this place.

As we could not march many miles in a day, through the feverity of the weather, bad roads, and the fhortnefs of the days, I am enabled to give you fome little defcription of the country between this city and Quebec.

Both

Both fides of the river are very well settled, which affords a pleafing profpect. The farms moftly lie clofe to the waterfide, and at fome diftance from each other, fo that each farmer has his poffeffions entirely diftinct from thofe of his neighbour's. But had an edict, which was paffed in the year 1745, when this province was under the French Government, been obferved, it would have been one continued ftreet from Quebec to this place, as it forbade the Canadians from extending their plantations more than an acre and a half in front, and thirty or forty acres in depth; by which means indolent heirs would not have waited for the inheritance of their fathers, as they would have been under the neceffity of forming new plantations, and fuch vaft fpaces of wood would no longer have feparated them from each other.

But whether that indolence they then poffeffed proceeded from nature, or the rigor of their Government, they feem now to have entirely loft it, and are become more induftrious; as I perceived, in many places, they were clearing away the woods to form new plantations.

Moft of the farm houfes are built of ftone, confifting of three or four rooms, which are heated with a ftove, nearly upon the fame conftruction as thofe I defcribed to you. Some of them have orchards annexed, though in general they are without fuch an accommodation, but all have exceeding good kitchen gardens.

Every three leagues there is a church, with a kind of little village, confifting of the parfonage, the *auberge*, the fchool for boys and girls, and a few houfes belonging to tradefmen, thofe but few indeed,

and

and so thinly scattered, that it scarcely gives you the idea of a village. Trade is considered by any descendant of the *noblesse* a disgrace, yet there are few inhabitants but what claim some affinity to one *Seigneur* or another, who, though they think it no derogation to plough, sow, and reap upon their plantations, deem it ignominious in the extreme, to be a mechanic or tradesman. Notwithstanding which, I was much surprized to find, that the principal inhabitant in each village, who generally belongs to some *noblesse*, was the post-master, and kept the only *Auberge* in the place; nay, did not think his nobility offended, with providing horses and entertaining travellers, which I remember to have heard you say is the case in many parts of Italy.

Between each church, or village, there are several crosses put up on the road-side, parallel to the shores of the river, and which

which are common throughout Canada. They are made of wood, about fifteen or twenty feet high, and proportionably broad: In that side towards the road is a square hole, in which they place some wax images, either of our Saviour on the cross, or of the holy Virgin, with the child in her arms, and before that, a piece of glass to prevent its being injured by the weather. These crosses are ornamented with all the instruments they think the Jews employed in crucifying our Saviour, such as the hammer, tongs, nails, a flask of vinegar, with many more things than one would suppose were really made use of, or even invented; and frequently the figure of a cock is placed at the top, which appeared to me rather singular, as it could have not the least affinity to the crucifixion, and must rather be supposed an allusion to the cock's crowing when St. Peter denied our Saviour.

These

These crosses, however good the intention of erecting them may be, are continually the causes of great delays in travelling, which to persons not quite so superstitiously disposed as the Canadians, are exceedingly unpleasant in cold weather; for whenever the drivers of the calashes, which are open, and nearly similar to your one horse chaises, come to one of them, they alight, either from their horses or carriage, fall on their knees, and repeat a long prayer, let the weather be ever so severe.

The usual mode of travelling is in these calashes: in the front of those which travel post, a man sits to drive, and who, let your business be of ever so great importance, will alight at these crosses, and pay his accustomed homage.

One day, on our march, being sent forward to procure quarters, with our friend

Captain Grattan, whose pleasantry of manners you are well acquainted with; for expedition we went in a post-calash. The weather was so excessively severe, that with the assistance of fur coverings, we could scarcely keep ourselves warm. Not above a mile had been beguiled, before we came to one of these crosses, when the fellow who drove us stopped; upon asking him why he did so, he replied, *Ce n'est que pour faire une petite prière*; which *petite prière* he was nearly five minutes in repeating, when he mounted his seat. We complained of being almost perished with cold, when he replied, *Allons, allons, je vais me depêcher*, and after taking two or three whiffs of his pipe, whipped up his horses, and made amends for his stopping. We had not gone a mile and a half further, before another cross made its unwelcome appearance: here he must alight, and *faire une autre petite prière*, which, upon our not consenting to, he begged we would let him

just

just stop, *le tems de faire un signe de croix*, which he was not long about. We then jogged on again with great chearfulness, as he drove pretty fast; soon after we perceived the village to which we were destined for quarters, when again he suddenly stopt, and upon our saying there was no cross there, he immediately cried out, *Mais en voici une la*, which, being at some distance from the road, we had not observed, requesting us to let him halt but a moment: *Il faut que je descende ici ; c'est mon village*; we told him he should not, and that he must drive into the village as fast as he could. Upon this he growled inwardly, and complained openly, till he came opposite to it, where he stopped again; before he could descend, our friend Grattan laid hold of his long queue, of which I told you they are exceedingly proud, and declared, if he did not immediately drive on, he would instantly cut it off.----
This being asserted with some degree of
warmth,

warmth, he thought fit to facrifice his religion to his vanity, fo juft croffing himfelf, muttered a fhort prayer, and drove us as faft as he could to the end of our journey, *facrant contre* the Englifh officers; and I do not doubt, if one could form any idea from his countenance, but he fent us both into purgatory with fuch curfes, that all the maffes which could be offered would not be able to releafe us from it, for having treated his religion and his queue with fo little ceremony.

Leaving you to make your own reflections on thefe Canadians and their religion, I remain,

Yours, &c.

LETTER XI.

Montreal, Nov. 20th, 1776.

MY DEAR FRIEND,

I SHALL now proceed with my obfervations, and the remainder of the occurrences which happened in our march from Quebec to this place.

About half way between Quebec and Montreal, is a town called *Trois Rivieres*; it takes its name from three rivers, whofe currents join here, and fall into the river St. Laurence. Previous to my giving you any defcription of this place, permit me to relate a trifling circumftance that occurred, juft just as we entered the town. About half a mile before we came to it, fo fudden and naufeous a fcent affailed our olfactory nerves, as nearly to fuffocate us, which lafted till we arrived at the outfkirts.--- Upon enquiry, we found it arofe from an animal, which the Canadians call the *Enfant du Diable*, or *bête puante*; a title which it derives from its ill fcent, occafioned by difcharging his urine whenever he is attacked, and which infects the air for a great diftance. Laying afide this quality, it is in other refpects a beautiful creature, being about the fize of a cat, with a fine fhining fur, of a dark grey color, ftreaks of white gliftening from the head to the tail, which is bufhy, like that of a fox, and turned up as a fquirrel's: this had been purfued by fome dogs which the foldiers had with them, acrofs the road, but when it came near us, its ftench was almoft infupportable.

Thefe

These *Enfant du Diable* differ from your *Enfant du Diable*, the London beaux, who have all their prettyisms perhaps, but are *eternally* exhaling their pestiferous odours, fearful, if they reserved them till *pursued*, they would have no opportunity to

" Taint the flying air, and stink in state."

The country is pleasant, and there are several good houses about the town, but they were greatly damaged by the Americans, upon abandoning it, after their defeat this summer, when their army was routed, and several of their Generals, with great numbers of their men, taken prisoners. This place is the winter cantonments of the German troops, who are commanded by General Reidesel; he commands likewise the district between Quebec and Montreal.

This town, by reason of the three rivers, used to be much frequented by the several nations

nations of Indians, and was built with a view of encouraging trade with the northern ones in particular. It had every profpect of being the fecond city in the province, but the fur trade was foon diverted from this market, and carried entirely to Montreal, it being fome leagues nearer to the Indians; and though we have feveral trading places with them upon the lakes Ontario and Superior, Montreal will always fupport its confequence, as being the neareft and moft convenient place for fhipping the furs to England. *Trois Rivieres* has now loft all its traffic and is fupported chiefly by the travellers paffing between the two cities.

There are feveral churches, and two convents, the nuns of which are reckoned the moft ingenious of any in Canada, in all kinds of fancy ornaments, needle work, and curious toys.

During

During my ftay at *Trois Rivieres*, there came down from the *Illinois*, feveral Indians of that nation, with an interpreter, to acquaint us, that they would be down in the fpring, and would take up the hatchet in favor of "*their good Brother who refided beyond the great waters.*" Among the groupe I obferved one, who had hanging round his neck the image of the holy Virgin, with our Saviour in her arms, which I thought very fingular, as he was of a nation efteemed extremely ferocious in their manner, and whom the French Miffionaries could not convert; but upon my enquiring of the interpreter if he knew the reafon, he gave me the following account:

In fome fkimirfh, when the *Illinois* were at war with the Canadians, this image had fallen into their hands, amongft other plunder. Sometime afterwards as a Miffionary, of which the French had great numbers

numbers travelling through the interior parts of Canada, to cultivate friendſhip, and eſtabliſh their religion among the Indians; by chance he met this perſon, and obſerving the image, was very much aſtoniſhed; the manner in which he took notice of it, excited the curioſity of the poor ſavage, to know what it repreſented, when the Miſſionary, who no doubt was pleaſed to have ſuch an opportunity of diſplaying his religion, told him, that it repreſented the mother of his God, and that the child ſhe held in her arms repreſented God himſelf, who had made himſelf man for the ſalvation of the human ſpecies, and explaining to him the myſtery of our incarnation, aſſuring him, that in all dangers the Chriſtians addreſſed themſelves to this holy mother, who ſeldom failed to extricate them. The Indian liſtened with the utmoſt attention to this diſcourſe, and went away.

Being out a hunting, foon after this, juft as he had difcharged his piece at a deer, one of the *Outagami* Indians, whofe nation was at variance with the *Illinois*, and who was lying in ambufh, prefented his piece at his head. In this fituation he recollected what had been told him about the mother of God, and invoked her protection. The *Outagami* endeavoured to difcharge his piece, but miffed; he cocked a fecond time, and the fame thing happened five times fucceffively. In the interim the *Illinois* had loaded his piece, and prefented it to the *Outagami*, who chofe rather to furrender than be fhot. From that time the *Illinois* would never ftir from his village without his fafeguard, which he imagines renders him invulnerable. There can remain little doubt but this circumftance was the means of his converfion to Chriftianity, and the Romifh religion: for he has certainly embraced that perfuafion, as I followed him to the great church, where, upon his entrance, after croffing himfelf with the holy water, he fell upon his knees, and feemed to worfhip with as much devotion as the moft devout of the Canadians. But to return to my defcription of this place.

The road from Quebec hither is the whole way within fight of the river, being moftly upon its banks, which renders it extremely pleafant to travellers, efpecially in the fummer, as there is a conftant breeze.

The river from Quebec to *Trois Rivieres* is very wide, and at that place it forms a very large lake, called *St. Pierre*, where the eye cannot reach acrofs; you can only difcern a large body of water, with feveral iflands, which, with the fmall veffels failing between them, form a very romantic profpect. The tide comes no farther than this lake, terminating a few leagues beyond

beyond *Trois Rivieres*, when you meet with the river again, where it runs extremely rapid, at the rate of seven or eight miles an hour. At its first appearance you can hardly suppose it the same river, for where the tide has effect, it seldom runs more than four miles an hour; it increases in rapidity as you advance to Montreal; and opposite the city it runs almost ten miles an hour, which renders its navigation extremely difficult, as nothing but a very strong and favourable wind, with all the sails full set, can enable vessels to stem the current. What with unfavourable winds and light breezes, ships have been as long in getting up from *Trois Rivieres* to Montreal, as they were on their passage from England to Quebec.

The rapidity of the current makes crossing not only disagreeable, but very dangerous, for unless you have a skilful pilot, the current will carry you a league below

I 2   where

where you want to land. And yet it is furprizing, how expert the Canadians are with their wooden canoes; but the Indians far exceed them in working theirs, as their canoes are of a much lighter conftruction. Both being much ufed in this country, I fhall endeavour to defcribe them, that you may be able to form fome idea of what they are.

Thofe which the Canadians ufe, are called wooden ones, being hollowed out of the red elm, fome of which are fo large, as to contain twenty perfons.

Thofe which the Indians ufe, are made of the bark of the birch tree, and diftinguifhed by the name of birch canoes, the different parts of which they few together with the inner rind of the bark of the tree, and daub them over with a pitch, or rather a bituminous matter, refembling pitch, to prevent their leaking. They form the ribs

from

from the boughs of the hickory tree, and are conftructed of different dimenfions, fome being only large enough to contain two perfons, and others thirty.

Thefe canoes are eafily managed by the Indians with their paddles, and with the current go at a prodigious rate, for one fingle ftroke with the paddle will force them twice the length of the canoe againft it. It was with one of thefe birch canoes that General Carleton, with an Aid-de-Camp, made their efcape through the enemy's fleet, when he quitted Montreal, for the purpofe of putting Quebec in a better ftate of defence.

Unwilling to lofe the opportunity of fending this by an officer who is going to Quebec, I am obliged to put a period to this letter: and, no doubt, upon the perufal of it, you will eafily difcover the young traveller, who is diverted with every thing that prefents itfelf to his view. But in hopes that it may afford you half an hour's amufement, I remain,

Yours, &c.

LETTER XII.

Montreal, November 26th, 1776.

MY DEAR FRIEND,

BEFORE I describe to you this city, let me give you some account of the island on which it stands, and from whence it derives its name.

This island, which measures, ten leagues in length and about four in breadth, is formed by the river St. Laurence, and in the center of it are two large mountains, which are the first you meet with on the north side of St. Laurence, and were called by the first discoverers of this province,

Monts Royaux, which gave name to the ifland, afterwards *Mont Royal*, and at laft, by a variety of corruptions of the language, *Montreal*.

Of all the adjacent countries, there is no place where the climate is reckoned to be fo mild, fo pleafant, and the foil fo fruitful: with all thefe natural bleffings, is it not furprizing to fee it thinly inhabited, and very ill fettled, for except two or three miles round the city, the country is moftly woods, interfperfed with a few fmall plantations.

One thing not a little remarkable is, that this ifland contains a fmaller one of about three miles in length, and two and a half in breadth, formed by two inlets of St. Laurence. This little ifland, which is called the *Ifle de Jefus*, is almoft cleared from woods, and has a fmall church and a few houfes on it, rendering Montreal

treal extremely pleasant; being so situated, that you cannot go a great length in any direction, before you come to it; and surely, after travelling through woods and swamps, it affords a most pleasing relief.

The summit of the mountains I have described to you are extremely difficult to gain; but having once accomplished it, the delightful prospect that presents itself, amply compensates for the fatigue and dangers you encounter, being able to view the whole island, and several leagues round it. You can plainly discern the mountains that cross *Lake Champlain*, called the Green Mountains, which are near 60 miles distant. It appears generally a vast forest, there being only three objects to diversify the scene: the view of the city of Montreal, the river St. Laurence, and the mountains of *Chamblée*, which are exceedingly beautiful, and the more remarkable, being in a plain level country, and
not

not having a single hill for several leagues round them; they are considerably loftier than the mountains on this island.

This city forms an oblong square, divided by regular, well formed streets, and the houses in general are well built; there are several churches, but those, as well as many of the houses have felt the effects of this war.

The city is surrounded by a wall and dry ditch, and at one end there is a citadel. These fortifications were raised many years past, as a defence against the Indians, and since the war, great improvements have been made to them; but the city is so situated, that no works can be raised to enabled it to stand a regular siege, having many rising grounds, that command it in more places than one.

When

When we gained poſſeſſion of this province, Montreal was nearly as large as Quebec, but ſince that time it has ſuffered much by fire; it is greatly to be wondered at, that it has not, one time or other, been totally deſtroyed: for in the winter, when the inhabitants go to bed, they make great fires in their ſtoves, and leave them burning all night, by which means they are frequently red hot before morning. Imagine how very dangerous they muſt have been, when their houſes were conſtructed of wood; few of thoſe are now remaining, except in the outſkirts of the city; the greateſt part of them being built of ſtone.

The inhabitants here, as well as thoſe of Quebec, having ſo many times ſuffered by fire, conſtruct their buildings in ſuch a manner, that they are not only perfectly ſecure againſt that element, but even againſt houſe-breakers, which being a little ſingular,

singular, you will have no objection to my describing them.

The house consists of one lofty floor, built with stone, and the apartments are divided by such thick walls, that should a fire happen in one of them, it cannot communicate to any other: the top of the house being covered with a strong arch, if the roof which is over it should catch fire, it cannot damage the interior part of the house. At Quebec, that city having been so often besieged, the inhabitants who are now building at that place, make this arch bomb-proof.

Each apartment has a double door, the inner one of wood, and the outer one of iron, which is only shut when the family retire to rest; the windows have double shutters of the same materials, and have not only taken this precaution with the doors that lead out of the house, but added

added an iron one, which is fixed on the infide.

Thefe doors and fhutters are made of plate iron, near half an inch thick, which, perhaps, you will imagine, muft give the houfe a very difagreeable appearance, but it is far otherwife, for being moftly painted green, they afford a pleafing contraft to the whitenefs of the houfe.

This is the bufy time of the merchants belonging to this place, who are now ufing all poffible expedition in fending home their furs, before the winter fets in. The reafon affigned for deferring it till fo late in the feafon, is on account of the traders, fome of whom are but juft arrived from the upper countries, the merchants generally waiting as long as there is a poffibility of their return, and fometimes fo long in expectation of them, as to lofe their markets entirely.

Thefe

These traders, in the course of their voyages, are continually encountering hardships and difficulties, and their lives are frequently in imminent danger:----- nothing can counterbalance the great perils that await them, but the certainty of acquiring an ample fortune in the course of three or four voyages.

They set out in the spring of the year, in parties of about twenty or thirty persons, with perhaps eight or ten large birch canoes; they have no fixed course to take, but steer that where it is imagined they can meet with a tribe of Indians; keeping mostly upon the upper lakes, sometimes carrying their goods and canoes across rapids, which are parts of the river greatly quickened by the descents, and over land to a river, up which they will proceed many leagues. If they do not meet with any Indians, it obliges them to return again to the lake, and proceed westward.

The

The goods they take with them to barter for skins, confist chiefly of brandy, tobacco, a fort of duffil blanket, guns, powder and balls, kettles, hatchets and tomahawks, as likewife looking-glaffes, vermillion and various other paints; and according to any article that an Indian has a defire or an ufe for, he will give ten times its value in fkins. They are moft eager after powder, ball, paint, brandy and tobacco.

Thefe traders traverfe vaft lakes and rivers with incredible induftry and patience, carrying their goods among nations in the remoteft parts of America. They are generally abfent from their families about three years, before their departure make a will, and fettle all their affairs, many of them, with their whole party, having been put to death by the Indians, either for the ftores they carry with them, or to revenge the death of fome
of

of their nation, who has been killed by the burfting of a gun that has been fold to them, which is frequently the cafe, they being by no means proof. The Indians do not wait for thofe traders who fold the gun, but take their revenge upon the firft they meet with. Here I muft obferve to you, that the guns which are fold to the Indians are fitted up in a very neat manner, to attract the notice of thefe poor creatures, and frequently, after having been fired five or fix times, they burft, and the unfortunate purchafer is either killed, or lofes an hand or an arm. Thefe traders are certainly the beft judges, but I cannot help thinking it both cruel and impolitic.

It having been hinted, that a reward would be given to him who fhould difcover a north-weft paffage, or whether the Continent joins to India, two fuppofitions much credited by the Europeans in general; feveral of the traders have endeavoured to find

find which is the true one: as there is every year fome frefh difcovery made, there remains but little doubt that in fome future time it will be effected. I believe the fartheft that any of them have yet reached was a Mr. Henry, who is reported to have travelled for ten days upon a large plain, on which grew only a rank-grafs, nearly as high as a man's breaft, and on this plain he frequently met with immenfe droves of buffaloes, and obferved the tracks of feveral others; that on the eleventh day he came to a vaft river, which ftopped his progrefs, as he did not chufe to venture crofling in a canoe; that the water was quite falt, and run extremely rapid, from which circumftance he concluded there muft be a north-weft paffage.

Whether it is fo or not, it is to be hoped that when this unhappy conteft is ended, Government may think it a matter worthy their confideration, and fit out an expedition

tion for afcertaining it, as the difcovery would not only be of great importance to England, but to all the world. As we have already made fuch great and wonderful difcoveries in the South Seas, furely this will be deemed of fufficient importance to juftify the expence of fitting out proper perfons from England to inveftigate the fact.

If after fo many fruitlefs attempts, fome one fhould appear, whofe firm mind will rife fuperior to every fenfe of danger, encountering variety of hardfhips, and whofe patience is not exhaufted by their duration; if fuch a one, animated with a hope of glory, which alone teaches men to difregard life, rendering them equal to the greateft undertakings; who, being well informed, fo as to underftand what he fees, and of veracity enough to relate only what he has feen---if fuch a man fhould appear, and no doubt there are many who poffefs
thefe

these excellent and extraordinary qualifications, his researches will perhaps be crowned with better success. But, if after such an undertaking, this celebrated passage should still remain concealed, it must be concluded, either that it doth not exist, or is not given to man to discover.

I add nothing more to this letter, fearful of losing its conveyance, therefore remain

Yours, &c.

LETTER XIII.

Montreal, Nov. 30th, 1776.

MY DEAR FRIEND,

A FEW days ago, I made a visit to our friend Shlagell of the 21st regiment, at St. John's, where he is stationed for the winter. I cannot but say I was much pleased with the place, it having all the appearance of a dock-yard, and of being equally as busy. The fleet that was upon the Lake is repairing, as likewise several of the vessels that we took from the Americans; they are laid up in docks, to preserve them from the inclemencies of the winter, and by the ensuing spring, what with the

ships

ships we had before, and those we have since taken from the Americans, we shall have a fleet far superior to any they can possibly bring on the Lakes.

There are two schooners here, the *Carleton* and *Maria*, which were built in England upon a construction to take into pieces, in order to be transported acrofs a carrying-place of about two miles. After their sailing from England to the mouth of the rapids, which prevented their proceeding up to St. John's, rather than lose the time of taking them to pieces, and re-constructing them, Lieutenant Schank, of the navy, an ingenious officer, informed General Carleton, that they might be conveyed upon a cradle over land to St. John's, entire, provided there was a good road made for them. The General acquiesced in this gentleman's proposal, and the whole army were employed in making a road. One of the vessels was near half a mile on it, by means

means of cables fixed to windlaſſes every twenty yards; but the General perceiving this mode of conveyance would take up more time than the other, gave orders to have the ſchooners taken to pieces and rebuilt, which was accompliſhed in as ſhort a ſpace of time as they had been creeping that ſmall diſtance upon land.

Our naval force being far inferior to what the Americans had this ſummer upon the Lakes, it was deemed neceſſary to encreaſe it. The ſhip-wrights were inſtantly employed to build a frigate, and the army in cutting the timber for it, which is now as complete a veſſel as any in the King's ſervice. I am afraid you will think I uſurp the privilege of a traveller, when I tell you that this frigate was conſtructed in ſo ſhort a time, that in eight and twenty days after her keel was laid ſhe was in action; and what was ſtill more wonderful, there were only ſixteen ſhip-wrights to build her, one
of

of whom was, on the third day, so badly wounded with an adze, as to be of little service.

You may easily imagine how great must have been the astonishment of the Americans when she came upon the Lakes, knowing we had no such ship when they abandoned St. John's. Notwithstanding this, they fought their fleet bravely, and our new-built vessel, by the falling of the wind, bore but a partial part of the engagement, the stress laying upon the *Carleton* and *Maria* schooners, which were both much shattered. On board the latter was General Carleton, who had a very narrow escape, a cannon shot passing close by him as he was giving directions to an officer, and which the General with that coolness and intrepidity that so much distinguishes his character, took no notice of, but turning round, gave his orders with as much compofure as if he had been in the moſt perfect ſtate of fecurity.

This place, which is called the key to Canada, when the works are compleated, will be of great ſtrength; there are temporary barracks at prefent, both for foldiers and artificers. The old barracks, as well as the fort the Americans deſtroyed when they abandoned the place, were formerly quite furrounded with woods, but are now clear for fome diſtance round.

In order that you may form a juſt idea of this important place, I have enclofed you a drawing of it, reprefenting the two redoubts, with the rope-walk, the ſhip on the ſtocks, and the other veſſels at anchor near the fort, and which I have taken from the block-houfe erected on the oppofite fide of the river Sorell,

From

From this place I went to the *Isle au Noix*, which is the advanced post of the army, on which the 20th regiment is stationed. This island is about a mile and a half in length, and three quarters of a mile in breadth; it was entirely covered with wood, but at present greatly cleared, and before the winter is over, we imagine it will be entirely so. Although so late in the year, and in this severe climate, the regiment stationed there is encamped, and likely to continue so till after Christmas, as it will be that time before the block-houses intended for them are finished.

Block-houses not being generally known in England, shall be my apology for giving you a description of them. They are constructed of timbers, placed one on the other, of a sufficient thickness to resist a musquet shot, and large enough to contain from 100 to 120 men; there are two apartments in them, one above the other,

in

the upper of which is a divifion for the officers. In both the lower and upper apartments are two pieces of cannon and four port-holes, for the purpofe of pointing thefe cannon on any fide of the blockhoufe on which it may be attacked; and in cafe an enemy fhould in the night endeavour to fet fire to the houfe, there are loop-holes, through which the troops on the infide can level their pieces and fire upon the affailants. They are reckoned to be a very ftrong defence, as it has been known that a fmall party of men, in one of thefe block-houfes, have repulfed treble their own number. But that you may more fully comprehend the conftruction of thefe unufual fortifications, I have inclofed a drawing and fection of one of them for your infpection.

The foldiers, not only at the *Ifle au Noix*, but likewife at St. John's, have been very fubject to the fcurvy, not having any

other

The Elevation and Plan of a Blockhouse.

Fig. 1.

REFERENCE.
Fig. 1.
A. The Port holes for Cannon.
B. The loop holes for Muskets.
C. The Door.
D. The fire places.
E. The Ladder of Communication to the upper Story.
F. The Trap Door.
G. The platform that serves as a parapet, and for the Men to stop on.

Fig. 2.
1. The Port holes for Cannon.

REFERENCE.
Fig. 3.
The Plan of the upper Story.
A. The port holes for Cannon.
B. The fire place.
C. The trap Door.
D. The platform as in the lower Apartment.
E. The Officers Apartment.
F. The Door leading to it.
G. The Window.
H. Slits made in the floor to fire upon the Enemy, if they gain the Entry of the Tower.

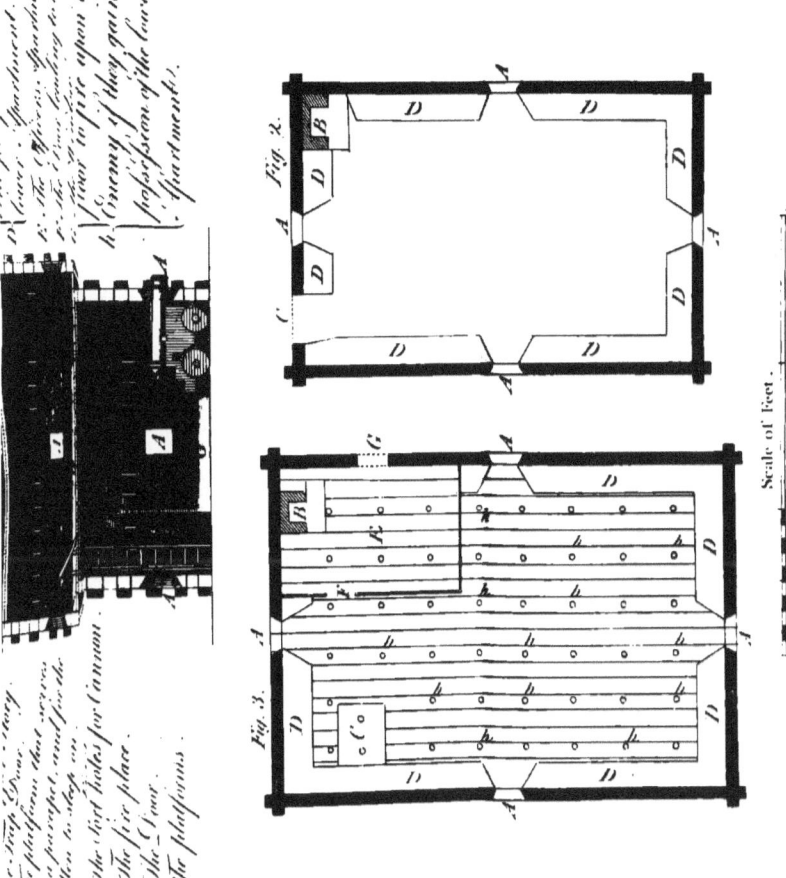

The Section and Plan of a Blockhouse.

other than falt provifions, but by drinking plentifully of fpruce beer, they are now all in perfect health, which clearly proves that liquor to be a powerful antifcorbutic. It is fo much known in England, as to need no defcription; the only difference between the fpruce there and here is, that here it is made with the branches of the tree itfelf, and there with the effence.

As the feverity of the weather fhuts up all intercourfe by letters, this is the laft you may expect to receive from me till the froft breaks up. But though I cannot write to you, be affured I fhall continually think of you, and remain, with the greateft efteem and fincerity,

Yours, &c.

LETTER XIV.

Montreal, January 18*th*, 1777.

MY DEAR FRIEND,

I DID not expect to have written so soon, but an opportunity of a flag of truce, which is going by the way of Ticonderoga to New-York, unexpectedly occurring, I am happy to embrace it, especially when it is impossible for me to employ my leisure hours more satisfactory to myself, than in endeavouring to divert you. I shall therefore proceed to give you some account of the winter amusements of this place, and among the principal ones is that of carioling upon the ice, the inhabitants
making

making large parties every day for that purpose; they generally go to *Point aux Trembles*, about three leagues from this city, at which place resides a Dutch woman, who makes most excellent sausages, and at whose house it is customary to refresh with these and bottled porter. As the north wind generally blows very sharp, you acquire a pretty good appetite, and, for my own part, I enjoyed this *petite repas* in preference to my dinner, very few regimental messes being conducted with that propriety and decorum which should characterize the profession, as there are generally among them a set of ungovernable young men. But to return to my description of carioling.

You will no doubt think it too much to go nine miles and back again for a jaunt before dinner; but this mode of travelling is so very expeditious, that most of the inhabitants defer their journey to Quebec till

till this feafon of the year, as they can perform it with lefs difficulty, and much greater expedition.

The carioles are fafhioned after different devices, to imitate birds and beafts, but in general they are of one conftruction, with only this difference, that the common people have theirs clofe upon the ice or fnow, while thofe of their fuperiors are raifed upon what are called runners, which elevate them about two feet. They paint them of various fantaftical colors; many of them, as a contraft to this feafon of the year, are colored in imitation of thunder and lightning. It is certainly a very eafy and expeditious method of travelling, for the horfes of the country will go with eafe fifteen miles an hour upon the ice. The inhabitants think nothing of a journey of forty or fifty miles to fee a friend, and returning the fame day.

Not-

Notwithstanding the river runs so rapid as I have before described, and is now entirely frozen over, yet there are certain warm springs that never will congeal; to caution travellers, every parish, as soon as the river is frozen over, is obliged to fix large pine trees in the ice, distant from each other about ten feet, which receiving moisture from the ice, and being an evergreen, continue so the whole winter, so that when travelling, it appears as if you were going between an avenue of firs.

On each side of the river it is quite smooth, but in the center, where the current runs so rapid, the ice is thrown up in prodigious hills, through which the inhabitants are obliged to cut a passage to cross the river; the sides are frozen so as to bear carriages, long before the center, and when that freezes, no thunder can equal the noise, the reason of which you will easily imagine, for where these rapids are, the

ice

ice is thrown up in a continual succession of hills; between these hills, you are surrounded with ice several yards high, and there it is inconceivably cold; when upon the top of one of these hills, you cannot help stopping to view the many curious forms the ice is thrown into, some of it being in that of a pyramid, other pieces that of a cone, others again in large slabs, and some of it resembling the figures of men, birds and beasts; in short, no description can equal so romantic a prospect.

The Canadians have a very singular custom among them, at the commencement of the year, the men go round the city and salute the ladies, who sit up in state for three days for that purpose, and as the inhabitants are acquainted with each other, the lady is generally saluted by the greatest part of the men; the salutation is after the French fashion, upon the cheek, when

having

having saluted one, the lady presents the other.

The European ladies who are settled here, rather than appear singular, adopt this custom, only varying the salutation after the English fashion; not but what I think the French mode preferable on this occasion, where the lady is under the necessity of receiving the salute of every one. As I know you will make this observation, *I dare say he went his rounds,* let me candidly acknowledge I did, and with another officer. We had a very great mortification in going to the house of an English merchant, who has a beautiful wife: upon our entering, we disputed who should salute her first; you may suppose how eager we both were in our addresses upon entering the room, and would have enjoyed our chagrin, when we saw General Phillips there, whose departure must be waited for, before we could salute the lady; perhaps you will say

say the pleasure was heightened by contemplating her charms---*Præstat expectare.*

This being the first Catholic country I ever was in, you must suppose me particularly attentive to their religious ceremonies at Christmas. I had ever conceived, that most authors had greatly exaggerated their accounts upon that head, and had I not met with convincing proofs, my candor could not suppose that mankind were so weak in their understandings. That the lower class of people should be led away is not to be wondered at, but how men of learning, sound sense and good understanding should, is to me astonishing. It is allowable for every man to worship any thing symbolically, but their doing it in reality never can be admitted. These superstitious people implicitly believe, the waxen images that are shewn them by their priests, to be absolutely the persons they are intended to represent.

On

On Christmas Eve, I went to the great church, where there was a prodigious concourse of people, and got as near as I could to the altar, to observe the ceremonies. About nine o'clock the service began with prayers and anthems, which lasted till ten, when the cradle was brought in, upon which there was a great shout; after this they continued singing and praying till the clock struck twelve, when the high priest brought in a wax figure of a child, superbly dressed, the music struck up, and there was a second great shouting. The child being deposited in the cradle, it was rocked till about one o'clock, when the ceremony finished.

In some of the convents they are exceedingly curious in their wax images: there was a representation of the Messiah, which was daily varied in its size, from the time of its supposed birth, till the time the Monks had fixed as necessary for its

being

being sufficiently grown to reprefent our Saviour, at the age he was when he preached in the Temple. When I firft went to fee this wax-work, on the Chriftmas-day, there was a figure of Jofeph, dreffed in a fcarlet cloak, with a large tie wig, another to refemble the Virgin Mary with a little child, laying in a manger, and over it was the figure an ox and an afs's head, which are at the fame time emblematical of their own ftubbornefs and ftupidity. In a few days this reprefentation was changed, and there was another of the Wife Men making their offerings to the *Salvator Mundi*; fo continuing every remarkable event of his life, till the time of preaching in the Temple; and whenever I went, there was always a vaft concourfe of people upon their knees praying to thefe figures. This mode of religion appears to me to be extremely well calculated to infpire devotion in the lower clafs of people, yet it is great pity fome better method of paying adoration

tion to the Divine Being cannot be adopted to infpire a true fenfe of his exiftence, than means fo abfurd. Difference of opinion concerning religion ever will prevail, but left you think I am growing too fermonic, I fhall conclude this fubject with an obfervation of a *Monfieur Blondeaux*, at whofe houfe I am quartered, and who is a very fenfible and intelligent man.

Converfing with him, one day, on their worfhipping thefe waxen images, and other ridiculous ceremonies in their religion, *Monfieur*, faid he, *Mon avis eft que chacun doit fuivre la religion pour laquelle il fe font plus d'inclination; et je fuis affuré qu'au jour du jugement, on ne nous demandra pas quelle religion nous avons profeffée, mais que nous ferons tous recompenfés on punis felon nos actions.*

As I informed you this goes by a flag of truce, it would be unpardonable to omit mentioning the humanity of General Carleton, who has cloathed all thofe who were taken prifoners, they being almoft in a ftate of nakednefs; many of them he fuffered to return to their homes upon their paroles of not bearing arms again during the war. Thofe who are here to be exchanged are cloathed, and fare the fame as our own foldiers.

Fate can only determine whether I fhall experience the misfortune of being taken prifoner, but, if I fhould, it is my hope that I may not meet with worfe treatment than thefe people have received.

By the mode this will be conveyed, I am not certain that it may reach you; but if it fhould, it brings you my beft wifhes for your health and happinefs, and an affurance that I am, with great fincerity,

Yours, &c.

LETTER XV.

Montreal, January 28th, 1777.

MY DEAR FRIEND,

THE winter is now set in with great severity, and you would naturally conclude that this country is the most uncomfortable in the world, and its inhabitants the most unhappy, but far from it: the city and the country people around, seem to be perfectly in their element; there is nothing but carioling, feasting, and other amusements. The Canadians perfectly resemble the French with respect to dancing, having meetings at each other's houses for that purpose almost every night.

Though the weather is so severe, the inhabitants here never stay in doors in the day, unless it snows, which seldom happens, for the first fall is generally the only one they have, and that lasts for two or three days, after which the weather is settled, and has been extremely pleasant for this month past; excepting one day, there has been quite an Italian sky, not a cloud to be seen.

The air of Canada is reckoned the most salubrious and healthy of any in the world; yet notwithstanding this, the Canadians are very consumptive, and it is incredible what numbers of them die before they arrive at maturity; if they survive that period, they mostly live to a good old age.

A very eminent physician, Dr. Kennedy, who is with our army, attributes this entirely to the stoves they make use of in the winter, and that was any other mode of

conveying

conveying warmth fubftituted, they would in all probability be a long lived people. For, fays he, the inhabitants moftly keep their ftoves heated, and in coming out of the frefh air to enter a room where there is one, you are almoft fuffocated. How pernicious this muft be to the conftitution, efpecially of the young children, who are continually going in and out of the heated rooms into the fnow and upon the ice; and when the lungs and pores are expanded by the heat of thefe ftoves, run without any addition of cloathing into the cold, where the blood receives fo fudden a change, that it generally leaves fome fatal diforder upon the lungs.

It is very difficult to eradicate long eftablifhed prejudices and cuftoms, but if the Canadians were to adopt the mode of other northern climates, where the cold is nearly as intenfe as it is here, I think they would experience the benefits arifing from it.

In

In Ruffia, Germany, and in all the northern parts upon the Continent in Europe, the inhabitants have ftoves fimilar to the Canadians, but fo conftructed, that when the room is of a fufficient warmth, the front opens with two folding doors, where there is a good fire in a grate, and the fulphureous air exhales up the funnel, by which means they enjoy an agreeable warmth; if they perceive it getting cold, they fhut the doors for a little while, till the room is fufficiently heated. The Canadian ftoves are fo conftructed, that the whole time you are in a room, you are almoft ftifled with the fulphureous vapor, which muft be extremely pernicious, and in all probability occafions the fallow complexion of the Canadians; there cannot be a ftronger proof that it is fo, than its having the fame effect on Europeans who have been fettled here any length of time.

They

They put me in mind of Erasmus's *Diverſoria Germanica*-----B. *In hypocauſto exuis ocreas; induis calceos; mutas, ſi voles, induſium, veſtes pluvia madidas ſuſpendis juxta hypocauſtum; ipſe te admoves, ut ſicceris. Itaque frequenter in idem hypocauſtum conveniunt octaginta aut nonaginta, pedites, equites, negotiatores, nautæ, aurigæ, agricolæ, pueri, fæminæ, ſani, ægroti.*---Gu. *Iſtuc verè cænobium eſt.*---Be. *Alius ibi pectit caput, alius abſtergit ſudorem, alius repurgat perones aut ocreas, alius eructat alium. Quid multis? Ibi linguarum ac perſonarum non minor eſt confuſio, quàm olim in turri Babel. Prodit famulus ſenex barbâ canâ, tonſo capite, vultu torvo, ſordido veſtitu.*---Gu. *Tales opportebat cardinalibus Romanis eſſe à poculis.*---Be. *Is circumactis oculis tacitus dinumerat, quot ſint in hypocauſto: quo plures adeſſe videt, hoc vehementius accenditur hypocauſtum etiamſi alioque ſol æſtu ſit moleſtus. Hæc apud illos præcipua pars eſt bonæ tractionis, ſi ſudore diffluant omnes. Si quis non aſſuetus vapori, aperiat rimam*

rimam fenestræ, nè præfocetur, protinus audit, Claude. *Si respondeas, Non* fero : *audis,* Quære igitur aliud diverforium.—Gu. *Atque mihi nihil videtur periculosius, quàm tam multos haurire eundem vaporem, maximè resoluto corpore, atque hic capere cibum, et horas complures commorari. Tum enim omitto ructus alliatos, et ventris flatum, halitus putres: multi sunt qui morbis ocultis laborant, nec ullus morbus non habet suum contagium.*---BE. *Sunt viri fortes, ista rident ac negligunt.*---Gu. *Sed interim multorum periculo fortes sunt.*---You will pardon me such a long quotation, but it is so apposite, that I could not resist it.

Although the weather is intensely cold, the mode of dress in use here, and these stoves, prevent your ever feeling any; there are none of those raw damp days, so much the subject of complaint in England, and from the bad effects of which no cloathing will defend you.

The

The dress of the natives is extremely well calculated for the climate; it consists (in addition to the common habiliments worn in England) of a blanket coat, a pair of what are called leggings, with a kind of flap on the outside of the leg, to prevent the snow from clogging round them; fur gloves, and a fur cap, which is made to pull over the ears, but this is seldom done, except when the strong north-west winds blow. At that time it is very dangerous to go out, as you run a great risque of being frost-bit, which happens in an instant, sometimes in turning the corner of a street, without being sensible of it at the time, as it occasions no sort of pain; if the part affected is not immediately rubbed with snow, and every precaution taken, it is sure to mortify, and should any one, thus circumstanced, be imprudent enough to go near the fire, mortification is inevitable.

To

To convince you how very inftantaneous it muft be, I fhall relate a ludicrous circumftance, which however had nearly been productive of a duel.

An officer in the garrifon having a nofe remarkably large, was going to dinner at the mefs, when not four doors from his lodgings, turning round a corner, he met another officer, who immediately cried out, " God blefs me, your nofe is froft-bit." From the fmall diftance he had gone, he thought it impoffible, and that his friend was bantering him; high words arofe, and they parted with an appointment to meet the next morning, to refent the affront. He made hafte to his dinner, and upon his entering the room, the officers prevented his coming to the fire, telling him at the fame time his nofe was froft-bit. He then began to think it no joke, and was happy to apply the ufual remedy : it was no bad punifhment for his rafhnèfs and incredulity,

lity, that during the time the officers were at dinner, he was obliged to be in the cold, rubbing his nose with snow till the blood circulated, and though very sharp set, obliged to nose a meal he would have been happy to partake of.

The present season of the year not permitting any military manœuvres, and naturally inclining us more to reflections of a serious nature, than the gay appearance of the spring or summer, I shall again trespass on your patience with some few observations on the effects of the intense cold weather experienced in this country; and as you have always appeared partial to my adding the remarks of others, where I thought them more just and beautiful than my own, I shall allude to some that struck me on the following phœnomena.

I have already mentioned to you that the frost is set in, and among the many inconveniencies

veniencies which the inhabitants of this northern region fuffer from it, none is more to be lamented than that of the ground being fo much frozen, as to make it impoffible to dig a grave for the interment of thofe who die at this time; their friends are obliged to keep them above ground till a thaw comes, when they return the body to the duft from whence it came.

You will eafily conceive, my dear friend, that the daily fight of fo mournful an object as the bier of a departed hufband, muft inevitably lengthen out the forrow of

> " The new made Widow—
> Whilft bufy meddling Memory,
> In barbarous fucceffion, mufters up
> The paft endearments of their fofter hours,
> Tenacious of its theme."

To relatives, who often think it a religious duty to mourn the departed, fuch fcenes, scenes, by a protracted sorrow, often draw life to its utmost verge, and at the funeral they are scarce more alive than the corpse they bury. To those who, without feeling a loss, are yet led to contemplate, it often suggests the idea of Arbuthnot,

"What am I? how produc'd? and for what end?
Whence drew I being? to what period tend?

I think you would hardly forgive me, were I not to relate to you the very strange manner in which these thoughts affect the German soldiers of our army. I know not whether to call it sympathy, or by any other name, but it strongly evinces the connexion existing between the body and mind.

The Germans, to the number of twenty or thirty at a time, will in their conversations relate to each other, that they are sure they shall not live to see home again, and are
certain

certain that they fhall very foon die: would you believe it, after this they mope and pine about, haunted with the idea, that

> " Nor wives, nor children, fhall they more behold,
> Nor friends, nor facred home."

Nor can any medicine or advice you can give them divert this fettled fuperftition, which they as furely die martyrs to, as ever it infects them. Thus it is that men, who have faced the dangers of battle and of fhipwreck without fear (for they are certainly as brave as any foldiers in the world), are taken off, a fcore at a time, by a mere phantom of their own brain. This is a circumftance well known to every one in the army.

In cafe of any deceafe in the family of a Canadian, the corpfe is depofited in fome private chamber, but in our general hofpital there is a long room appropriated for
that

that purpofe. The fuperintendant of this room, an apothecary, being a man poffeffed of whimfical ideas, and a turn for the ludicrous, had placed the dead bodies of thefe poor Germans in various poftures, fome kneeling with books in their hands, others fitting down with pipes in their mouths, many ftanding erect againft the wall, and as they have their cloaths on, you fcarcely at firft imagine they are dead; but upon a nearer approach, what with their long muftaches, which are put in form, and their ghaftly countenance, you cannot picture to yourfelf any thing fo horrible, yet at the fame time fo truly laughable and ridiculous.

After what I have related, you will moft probably agree with me, that the conftitution of England has not unwifely declared apothecaries and furgeons incapable of compofing a jury upon trials for capital offences

offences, though it excludes some few of them who do honor to the profession, by their gentleness and humanity: yet I am fearful the major part of them would not join in the warmth that is so frequently experienced, in the generous and noble bursts of joy that overwhelms the order of our courts of justice, when unprotected innocence escapes the arbitrary and revengeful prosecution of malice and power. I have heard surgeons, as an excuse for the strange want of feeling either brought on by the daily visitation of sickness and pain, or which they possess from the apathy of their nature, say, that were they to feel much on the occasion, it would disable them from doing their duty. Strange argument this! and as contradictory to sound sense as true philosophy, which might teach them gentleness in the manner, and firmness in the execution. For my own part, such is the situation of my mind, when I am indisposed, that I have fancied

the

the affectionate "how do ye" of the surgeon and apothecary, has done me as much good as their drugs, or the performance of an operation in phlebotomy. Can any one conceive it proper, when a youth of sixteen has broke a leg, that the surgeon, while in doubt on the first visit, should, in the presence of his patient, refuse to search whether a fracture had actually happened, because *he would make such a roaring and a noise that he should not get it out of his head for a fortnight*, and though the lad with spirit assured him, that those who were present had not seen him shed a tear; the surgeon, however, did not make the experiment, though I believe for a much better reason than he gave, which was that the leg was much swelled. Thus did a surgeon, while I was in England, treat our cousin B——, lowering his spirits, leaving him three or four days in suspence, whether his leg was broken or not, merely to shew how

coolly

coolly he could talk on a subject like that before him. Had he, instead of this unfeeling excuse, but tenderly assured his patient, that it would put him to more pain to make the search then, than at a future time, I should have supposed it would have made his mind more easy, and been the means of preventing the access of a fever, always to be feared on these occasions.

In the hospitals, perhaps the multiplicity of cases may plead an excuse for little ceremony, but in private practice, where they are well paid, thus wantonly to wound the feelings of those who are but in ill spirits, cannot add either to their credit or practice.

You will long ere this wonder how I have strayed from the wild scenes that surround me, to lash the hardened professors
of

of the Esculapian art, but you too well know that such things do exist, not to pardon my deviation. I shall therefore conclude with my sincere wishes that you may never have the misfortune to fall into their hands, and remain

Yours, &c.

LETTER XVI.

Montreal, February 27th, 1777.

MY DEAR FRIEND,

AS my laſt was liable to the inſpection of the enemy, I been have reſtrained from informing you of many things that it would otherwiſe have communicated. I embrace, therefore, the opportunity of an officer going to Quebec, in order that you may receive this by the firſt ſhip that ſails for England.

Since my laſt I have been again to St. John's, where, notwithſtanding the ſeverity of the weather, the artificers and ſhip-
wrights

wrights are all bufily employed. We have raifed upon the Lakes, in addition to the force of laft fummer, a curious veffel, called a *Radeaux*, which formerly belonged to the French, and was funk by the Americans near this place : it is a caftle of itfelf, of a monftrous conftructure, and will hold a great number of men; fhe is intended to convey the heavy artillery acrofs the Lakes. From the account, indeed, that we have received from fome deferters, the Americans do not intend to difpute them, **but wait our arrival at Ticonderoga.**

The garrifon at St. John's has been kept very alert moft of the winter, as feveral parties of the enemy have come acrofs the Lake upon fleighs, and having hovered about the woods, twice attacked the blockhoufe on the oppofite fhore, their views, no doubt, were of deftroying our fleet; but to render the fhips more fecure, the ice has been cut away for feveral yards round

round them, to prevent their being set fire to.

As I returned from St. John's along the river, my attention was suddenly caught by an object well calculated to have exercised the feelings, and employed the pen of a Sterne.

When the river freezes over, the Canadians cut a square hole in the ice, for the cattle to drink out of. I saw a drove of sheep surrounding one of these holes: the whole flock looked most piteously, and bleated with so mournful a lamentation, as would have pierced a heart of stone; one of them seemed infinitely more agitated than the rest, and exhibited feelings that would have done honor to the most tender sensibility. Curiosity, concern, or what you will, led me instantly to the mouth of the hole, where a poor little lamb, not four days old, urged by extreme thirst, had fallen

fallen in; it was struggling for life, and sent forth such distressful cries!---my God, how my pulse beat, and my breast was full, even to bursting!---how often did it get its little feet on flakes that seemed to promise it support, and as often it slipt back again into the water; now it seemed by ineffectual exertions, anxious for life, and now hopeless and despairing, lay inanimate;--- it was some time before I could extricate it; do me justice, and guess my feelings till I had effectually saved its life. I took it up in my arms, and the whole flock followed me to the farm house. To describe the mother's solicitude, and the joy at finding it safe, is impossible; language can never betray what the imagination itself can scarcely paint. You who are possessed of sympathy, and a tender regard for the whole creation, which is perhaps the greatest ornament of human nature, will easily believe the infinite pleasure this little office of humanity afforded me.

This

This is one of the many things in which the mind might be apt to arraign the wifdom of Providence, why nature fhould give birth to fuch tender creatures, at fo rigorous a feafon of the year, when to all appearance they require the utmoft warmth to bring them to perfection.

A few days fince I went to *Verchere*, to fee fome officers of the 24th regiment, which village is extremely pleafant, commanding a very extenfive view both ways of the river, with a profpect of this city. It derives its name from a circumftance, wherein it is proved that the fair fex, upon emergencies, poffefs a courage equal, if not fuperior to ours. In the year 1690, when this province was in a continual ftate of warfare with the Indians, and the inhabitants were obliged to refide in forts, it happened that a *Madame de Verchere* was left alone in the fort, whilft the reft of the people were at work in the fields; a fmall party

party of Indians gaining this intelligence, were determined to enter the fort, plunder it, and take her prifoner; *Madame de Verchere,* however, perceiving them approach in a pofture for fcaling the palifado, fired fome mufquet fhot, and drove them to a diftance; they inftantly returned, and were again repulfed, aftonifhed, you may be fure, fince they could only difcover a woman, who appeared as undifmayed as if fhe had been furrounded with a numerous garrifon. The Indians knowing the place was unprovided with any other defence, made feveral attempts, and were always repulfed by the lady, who defended herfelf in the fort for near four hours, with a valor and prefence of mind which would have done honor to an old warrior: they were at length compelled to retire entirely, as the inhabitants of the fort (who always went out to labor with their mufquets, in cafe of an attack) were returning, and greatly fuperior in number to the Indians. This

was

was not the only inftance of this lady's courage, for about two years after, a party of the fame Indians, but much more numerous, furprized and took prifoners the men, when at work; a little girl happened to make her efcape, who, running into the fort acquainted *Madame de Verchere* of what had happened. Shortly after the Indians appeared before the fort, leading the men captive. There was not a foul left in it, befides a young foldier and a number of women, who raifed moft lamentable cries at the fight of their hufbands being led prifoners. In the midft of this, *Madame de Verchere* loft neither her courage nor prefence of mind, for after locking up the women, that their groans and weeping might not infpire the Indians with additional courage, and affuming the habiliments of a foldier, fhe fired a piece of cannon and feveral mufquet fhot, fhewing herfelf with her foldier, fometimes in one redoubt and fometimes in another, always firing

firing upon the approach of the Indians to the breaft-work, who did not make a fierce affault, as by her ftratagem they fuppofed there were many men in the garrifon. Fortunately for the lady, fhe had not long to remain in this difagreeable ftate, for the *Chevalier de Crifafy* who was Governor of a fmall fort at *Chamblée*, upon hearing the firing of cannon, came to the fuccour of the place, and that fo fuddenly, that the Indians were obliged to make a very precipitate retreat, leaving their prifoners behind them.

This remarkable lady lived to a good old age, and died in Normandy, where there is a monument erected to her, with thefe two fingular inftances of her fortitude and bravery.

One would imagine that this fpot of *Verchere* was deftined for the trial of fortitude and bravery in the fair fex, to which I might

might add conjugal affection. At this time a lady refides here, noble by birth, in whom is united all the foftnefs and delicacy of her fex, ever accuftomed to thofe elegancies and refined enjoyments which are attendant upon high rank and fortune: fhe has forfaken all the pleafures of the gay and fafhionable world, to accompany her hufband to the wild forefts of Canada; already travelled a vaft extent of country, in different extremities of feafon, and with difficulties that an European will not eafily conceive. Such inftances of connubial attachment, in the levity of the prefent day, are rarely to be met with; but that fuch characters do exift, and that the pleafures and gaieties of the *beau monde* have not altogether vanquifhed the focial virtues, is to be inftanced in that pattern of her fex, Lady Harriet Ackland, who has not only encountered the hardfhips already defcribed, but upon joining the army, in addition to her former fatigues, had to attend her hufband

upon

upon his sick bed, in a miserable hut at *Chamblée.* A mind like hers, animated by love and affection, is alone capable of encountering such hardships.

General Phillips commands this garrison, and is much esteemed by the officers of the army; he gives them as little trouble as possible, but will have them perform their duty, and seldom misses coming upon the parade in a morning. The following anecdote will give you a trait of his character, and shew you the method he has of gaining the esteem of the officers:

One evening several young officers of the artillery having made a little too free with " the Tuscan grape, and being high in blood," went to the house of a Canadian, the father of three very pretty daughters: it happened the young ladies were at home, and as they had frequently given some little encouragement to the officers, these young

Vol. I.   N   men

men thought themselves warranted in taking a few liberties with them; but, as the wine had deprived them of all ideas of reftraint, they proceeded farther than the rules of decency or delicacy allow of, or than I chufe to relate. In the midft of this fcene the father arrived, whofe appearance added greatly to the confufion, and the old gentleman making a general alarm and outcry, the officers were obliged to decamp.

The next morning a formal complaint was made to General Phillips, by the father of the young ladies, who faid that if he was not immediately redreffed, he would fet off for Quebec, and lay his complaint before General Carleton, at the fame time informing him who had been the aggreffors, adding, with fome warmth, *Qu'il étoit bien certain que ce bon General lui rendroit juftice.*

The General profeſſed himſelf extremely ſorry that ſuch a diſgrace ſhould have fallen upon the officers of that garriſon, and that he ſhould, for his own ſake, render him all the juſtice in his power, in order to wipe off ſuch a ſtigma from his own corps, which pacified the Canadian.

The next day being the General's levee, thoſe officers, who were now become conſcious of their imprudent behaviour, did not abſent themſelves, leaſt it ſhould argue guilt. After the General had made his bow of retirement to the levee, he deſired that the officers of the artillery would remain, and the reſt of the company being departed, he addreſſed them in the following manner:

" Gentlemen, I have had a very heavy
" complaint made to me by one of the in-
" habitants, of ſome of the officers of the
" artillery, and cannot but ſay I feel it
" more

" more forcibly, as commanding that corps
" ---and of such a nature too---Gallantry
" has ever marked the soldier's character,
" and I could allow you to use every per-
" suasive argument that lays in your power,
" but for Heaven's sake, don't use violence,
" that is beneath a man!---For my own
" part, I do not know who has been guilty
" of such conduct, nor can I form the
" least idea of the person, unless it was
" Capt. H---, (pointing to an old and in-
" firm officer) I am sure it could not be
" any of the young gentlemen, certainly
" their persons and address would have
" ensured them success. When you solicit
" the fair, violence becomes unnecessary.
" I neither know who the officers were,
" nor do I wish to be informed; but let
" me advise them to pursue different means,
" when they next address the ladies, as
" they may rest assured those they have
" adopted will never succeed. I only desire
" that I may never hear of any more such
com-

"complaints, nor need I suggest to those
"gentlemen who are conscious of having
"been concerned in this affair, that it is
"compatible with their characters, to
"make every satisfaction and apology for
"their conduct, to the father of the young
"ladies."

I need not observe, that those who had been the cause of this handsome reprimand of the General's, immediately went and made the required apology. Thus, by the natural politeness and address of General Phillips, ended a business, which, under the cognizance of a more austere commander, might have been rendered fatal to the characters and fortunes of those who had erred only in the moment of inebriation.

Most of the inhabitants have large holes dug in their cellars, which they fill with ice, and those who have them are now laying

laying it in for the fummer. I am informed the heat is equally as predominant as the cold is at prefent, and were it not for the ice cellars, they could not keep their provifions fweet a day. At this feafon of the year, the inhabitants have very little trouble in going to market, having only the article of eggs and butter to purchafe, for as foon as the froft fets in, they generally purchafe what provifions they think will ferve them till it breaks up, not only flefh and fowl, but even fifh, for they make holes in the ice, and let down nets five or fix fathom long, which feldom are drawn up empty, and thefe articles, when brought for fale, are frozen as hard as a ftone; the provifions being laid in fo long before they have occafion to ufe them, are always tender. When they want to drefs any thing, it is put into a pail of cold water before the fire, otherwife the water would foon be congealed; in about an hour,

hour, whatever kind of provision is put in thaws, and becomes fit for use.

The lower clafs of Canadians are exceedingly infolent, and infult the officers upon every occafion; their behaviour would be infufferable, did they not now and then get feverely chaftifed. Was I induced to hazard an opinion as to the caufe of this, I fhould attribute it to the very great indulgence fhewn to them by General Carleton; they imagine it is only to lay their complaints, however abfurd, before him, and be redreffed, according to the ftory they tell him. The following is the beft fpecimen I can give you, in confirmation of my affertion:

As Colonel Carleton was driving his cariole, with a lady in it, upon the ice, a Canadian drove his fleigh defignedly againft the Colonel's cariole, by which it was overfet and much damaged: upon this the

Colonel gave him a moſt ſevere horſe-whipping, which the Canadian bore very patiently, ſaying with a ſlight ſhrug, *Fouëttez donc Monſieur, juſques a ce que vous ſoyez fatigué, mais je vous aſſure je m'en plaindrai au General Carleton.* The Colonel then encreaſed his flagellation, telling him at the ſame time, *Et quand vous vous plaindrez au Général, ayez la bonté de l'informer en même tems, que c'eſt ſon frère qui vous a fouëtté.* The Canadian hearing this, and preſuming he ſhould then obtain no redreſs, began to aſk pardon, became very ſubmiſſive, and was glad to make the beſt of his eſcape, by ſlinking away and drawling out, *Que ſ'il eut ſu que c'etoit le frère du bon Général, il n'auroit pas fait cela pour tout au monde.*

This little anecdote, while it convinces you what great lengths theſe plebeians go, when they imagine themſelves protected, will afford you an example of that meanneſs nefs ever attendant upon vulgar and bafe minds, when a proper chaftifement is beftowed upon them, for fuch inftances of their audacity.

I am juft informed there is an opportunity of fending letters to Quebec, from whence this will foon reach you, with my fincere wifhes for your health and happinefs. I remain,

Yours, &c.

LETTER XVII.

Montreal, April 6th, 1777.

MY DEAR FRIEND,

AS we are now in daily hopes of the froſt's breaking up, and every one is anxious and impatient to hear from his friends, do not let me meet with a diſappointment.

Being deſirous to viſit every place worthy of notice, I went to *Chamblée,* where are the remains of a fort, formerly built by by the French, for what purpoſe they are the beſt judges: it is ſaid their intention was to prevent an army entering Canada.

It

It is so situated, that an army can march by *La Prairé* and *La Chine*, take *Montreal*, and then turn their whole force against the fort, which would be thus cut off from any relief. This has been clearly evinced this war, when General Prescott, with several companies, were taken prisoners in it.

The fort is built of stone, of a regular square, with four bastions at each angle, without any out-works, and is situated a few miles from the mountains which I have already described; from its situation I can never suppose it otherwise than intended as a magazine for stores and provisions to supply St. John's.

About three miles from the fort are the rapids, which prevent shipping going up to St. John's; there is a saw-mill there, and it being the first of the kind I ever saw, I was particular in my examination of it.

After

After the owner had given me every necessary information, I afked him which Government he preferred, when he exclaimed, *Oh! Monfieur, il n'y a point de comparaifon, l'Anglois l'Anglois!* and then related a circumftance, which no doubt you will fay carried a powerful reafon for the poor old man's giving us the preference, and affords another proof how much the Canadians were oppreffed by the French.

There was a cuftom, which is continued for the repair of roads, tranfporting provifions, and other fervices for Government, called a *corvée*; it is in the breaft of the Captains of the Militia to nominate fuch a number of inhabitants to go with horfes and carts upon that duty.

At the time Lord Amherft was expected to enter Canada, acrofs Lake *Champlain*, the French were continually fending fupplies of ammunition and provifions to

Chamblée and St. John's, and the inhabitants, as well as their cattle, were almost worked and harrassed to death, by the oppression and tyranny of the Captains of Militia.

Before the campaign commenced, General Montcalm went to St. John's and *Chamblée*, to see that those garrisons were in a perfect state of defence, when the poor peasants assembled in a body round him, and fell on their knees to tell their grievances. The man who owned the sawmill told the General he was willing to serve *le Grand Monarque*, but he had been much oppressed; that his harvest and plantation had been neglected, and his family almost ruined and starving; and, to add to his misfortunes, *que le deux seuls chevaux qui lui restoient étoient morts de fatigue la veille*: to which the General, instead of comforting and redressing the poor old man, with a very stern look, and at the same time

time twirling his *croix de St. Louis*, replied, *Mais vous en avez les peaux, c'eſt beaucoup, c'eſt beaucoup!*

Among the various amuſements we enjoyed while away this long winter, I forgot to mention that ſkating is one, which thoſe who are fond of that diverſion are amply indulged in, there being ſuch a conſtancy and large extent of ice. There are ſeveral officers in the regiment, who being exceeding fond of it, have inſtituted a ſkating club, to promote diverſion and conviviality.

The Canadians ſkate in the manner of the Dutch, and exceedingly faſt, but the Indians dart along like lightning. Some years ſince, for a conſiderable wager, three Indians ſet off from this place at day light, and before dark arrived at Quebec, which is 60 leagues; their fatigue, however, was ſo great, that two expired ſhortly after their

their arrival, and the third did not furvive above a week.

In this country there is no fpring nor autumn, and as the froft is daily expected to break, the troops are kept in continual exercife. General Carleton is come to review the different regiments; but the fnow is fo deep upon the ground, they are exercifed and to be reviewed on the ice, which you would naturally think extremely dangerous, and that the men would flip and do one another mifchief with their bayonets; but fuch is the power of the fun at this time, that during the day it thaws the furface, which freezing again at night, forms a kind of fmall ice, affording a fteady footing, added to which, all the ice oppofite the city is covered with loofe ftraws blown from the dung. The foil being fo extremely prolific, they have no occafion for manure, and therefore bring
it

it in sleighs upon the ice, to be carried away when it breaks up.

There are many unpleafant duties attending an officer, but none more fo than fitting upon a court-martial. A few days ago, being upon that duty, I felt myfelf much diftreffed, as being the junior officer, and of courfe the firft to pafs fentence, but was foon releafed from that painful tafk, the culprit efcaping a punifhment, by his blunt oddity. The crime for which he was tried, and for which he had been twice punifhed before, was that of drunkennefs and diforderly behaviour, which being upon this occafion clearly proved, he was afked by the Prefident what he had to fay in his defence. He replied, " Oh! and plaife " your Honors, I have nothing to fay, but " to fave your Honors and the Court any " further trouble, you may fet me down two " hundred, I'm fure your Honors will think " that enough." The droll and fimple manner

ner in which the fellow fpoke, accompanied with his dialect, occafioned a fmile upon every one prefent. After he was ordered to withdraw, the Court were of opinion, that as the man was in other refpects a good foldier, his whimfical manner fhould in this inftance fave him a punifhment; when, being called in, and receiving a fevere reprimand from the Prefident, and his promifing never to be guilty of the like again, he was difmiffed. After thanking the Court for their lenity, he faid, " Since " as your Honors have been fo good to me, " I'll *keg* myfelf for fix months, directly I " get home." As you will not eafily comprehend the word *keg*, or how it can be applied in this inftance, I will explain it to you: it is a cant word that the foldiers have among them, when they wifh to refrain from liquors, they take an oath that for fuch a limited time they will not touch any fpirits whatever, and if they are ftrongly addicted to liquor, not hing can

Vol. I.   O   tempt

tempt them to tafte any. Perhaps you will fay, it would not be amifs if the officers fometimes followed their example.

It is incredible to think what a difference a few days makes at this feafon of the year. About fix days after our regiment was reviewed, the fnow began to thaw, and is now totally diffolved, except where there has been great drifts, and the ice along the banks has fuch great chafms, that the river is now unfafe to pafs over. The center, where the rapids had thrown up the ice, every now and then breaks, with a noife equal to thunder.

It is aftonifhing how quick vegetation is in this country, you can almoft perceive the grafs grow; the fnow has not been gone many days, and the fields are entirely green, which can only be attributed to the ground's being continually covered with fnow, which nourifhes and preferves
the

the blades with such a warmth, that when the sun, which even now is extremely powerful, can come at it, it brings it forward so very rapidly.

The roads are almost impassable, but I am informed that in the course of a fortnight they will be as dry and dusty as in the midst of summer.

In going out of the city towards *Point aux Trembles*, on the right hand, stand as stately old house, which was built by a person, who, after many disappointments and losses in trade, with the most unremiting and indefatigable industry, had scraped together a plentiful fortune, and as an allusion to the particulars of his life, had carved over his front door the figure of a dog gnawing a large fleshy bone, with this whimsical inscription:

> *Je suis le chien qui ronge l'os*
> *Sans en perdre un seul morceau :*
> *Le temps viendra, qui n'est pas venu*
> *Je mordrai celui, m'aura mordu.*

The great diverſion of carioling is now over, and the inhabitants are getting ready their calaſhes, for they are equally as fond of driving in them as in their carioles.

I am told there is ſeldom a winter paſſes, but ſeveral people loſe their lives, both before the river freezes over and when the ice breaks up, by being too adventurous in croſſing it, a ſhocking inſtance of which happened three days ago.

Acroſs the chaſms made by the ice in breaking up, which ſometimes are five or ſix yards wide, a bridge of planks is thrown; a cariole paſſing over one of theſe, in which was two perſons, the horſe proving unruly, drew it over the ſide, and they fell down the chaſm near forty feet, where they remained a little time, it being narrow at the bottom, and though every aſſiſtance was inſtantly had, no relief could be afforded, as before the ladders and ropes

could

could be let down to them, the weight of the horfe and cariole broke the ice at the bottom, and they were all carried away by the current.

I could not help thinking of the poor lamb in the fame fituation, and lamented the ftriking difference between the defpair of a whole anxious flock for the lofs of a young one, and that buftling coldnefs which difgraced humanity, at the fudden and unexpected death of a man.

The cloathing for the army not being fent out laft year, and as it will be too late to fit it to the men when it arrives, the commanding officers of the different regiments have received orders to reduce the men's coats into jackets, and their hats into caps, as it will be the means of repairing their prefent cloathing, and be more convenient for wood fervice, that when the army take the field, they will in a manner

ner be all light infantry. The regiments have the hair that is affixed to their caps of different colors; ours is red, and as the pureſt white hair takes the beſt color, ſeveral ſoldiers, ambitious to have theirs ſuperior to the reſt, occaſioned a very ludicrous affray betwixt them and the inhabitants, in which the ſoldiers were worſted, and got a ſevere beating.

They went into a field, to the number of about twenty, and began to cut the hair from the bottom of the cows tails: the owner obſerving this, aſſembled his neighbours and fell upon the ſoldiers with ſticks, when a ſcuffle enſued, and the ſoldiers returned home with broken heads.

Two that had been ſeverely beaten, made a complaint to the Major of the regiment, who aſked them if they had on their ſide-arms, when replying in the negative,

gative, he told them how glad he was they had got a beating; that they fhould always be worn, being the fame to a foldier as a fword was to an officer.

The inhabitants fay, that the winter has been quite mild to what the laft was, and if fo, their hard winters muft be terribly cold; that in general the froft feldom breaks till the end of this month, and fometimes May; and as a proof of its mildnefs, feveral nations of Indians have come fome hundred miles to join the army.

It is a pity their affiftance cannot be difpenfed with, as they will not be reftrained; they are abfolutely neceffary in this woody country, and efpecially as the enemy have them, they are a reftraint upon each other, and I really believe fo much mifchief will not enfue, as if only one party had engaged them. Thofe on our fide side will be superior in numbers to the Americans, as they cannot furnish them with necessary supplies.

The attachment of the Indian lasts no longer than you heap presents on him, and he sides with that party which will make the greatest.

It is absolutely necessary to keep well with them, for though there is such an amazing tract of country in possession of Europeans, it is nothing when put in competition with the unknown tract that extends to the westward. And though the Indians are much depopulated, still they are a very numerous race of people; it is altogether unknown where many nations are settled, nor could it be ascertained any such existed, were it not for straggling Indians belonging to them, that are casually met with.

These

These people are under great subjection to their chiefs, and pay implicit obedience to them: They come every year to Montreal, to what is called the fair, when several hundreds of them assemble, and are exceedingly troublesome to the inhabitants, they receive presents to keep them peaceable, and in league of friendship; it is incredible what immense sums it annually costs Government for that purpose.

General Carleton returns to-morrow to Quebec, and as I send this by one of his Aid-de-Camps, who is going to England, and who has sent his servant for my letters, I am obliged to conclude hastily, with assuring you, that you shall hear from me by every opportunity, and remain,

Yours, &c.

LET-

LETTER XVIII.

Montreal, May 20th, 1777.

MY DEAR FRIEND,

NOT having had a letter from you thefe fix months, it is impoffible to exprefs the pleafure yours gave me. I fincerely rejoice that your health is re-eftablifhed, and hope it will always continue fo.

You hint in yours, that great events are expected in the courfe of the enfuing campaign, and that the operations of the two armies will nearly terminate this unfortunate conteft. As to our army, I can only fay, say, if good difcipline, joined to health and great fpirit amongft the men, with their being led on by General Burgoyne, who is univerfally efteemed and refpected, can enfure fuccefs, it may be expected ; but, as I obferved before, we have more dangerous enemies at home, than any we have to encounter abroad, for all tranfactions that are to take place are publicly known, long before they are officially given out in orders, and I make no doubt but you will be as much furprized as the General was, when I tell you that the whole operations of the enfuing campaign were canvaffed for feveral days before he arrived, who no doubt fuppofed, that in giving out his orders he was communicating an entire fecret.

If, therefore, there are people in office, fo imprudent as to communicate any public intelligence, no doubt the numerous agents and well-wifhers to the Americans
will

will not be negligent in gaining continual and immediate information. As intelligence is the main fpring of every movement in an army, the Americans will have a great advantage, and what will add confiderably to that advantage, is the great fecrecy they obferve, and the utter impoffibility to obtain the leaft intelligence of any of their defigns, while they are previoufly acquainted with every one of ours.

About three weeks ago the river broke up, which was accompanied with a moft aftonifhing noife: it happened in the night, and you muft judge how ftrange it muft appear, after being ufed to fee, for fuch a length of time, fo fpacious a body of ice, with horfes, carriages, and men travelling on it, changed to a beautiful river, with a number of fhips and boats failing and rowing upon it.

The

The country wears quite a new face, and summer is come all at once. The inhabitants are now busily employed on their farms, and every thing appears a scene of bustle and industry, after such a length of time passed in dull inactivity.

The army is now in movement to take the field; the advanced corps are already encamped at *Boucherville*, and were reviewed by General Burgoyne a few days since. I accompanied several officers to see them, who had never seen 1500 military men assembled together. As to the battalions of the light infantry and grenadiers, such a body of men could not be raised in a twelvemonth, search England through. The line of the advanced corps extended a mile; they performed, exclusive of the common manœuvres, several new ones, calculated for defence in this woody country, and the General was pleased to express his approbation in the warmest terms,
with

with regard to the high difcipline of the men. They proceed in a few days to St. John's, and from thence they are to go upon the Lake, as far as the river *La Cole*, where they are to encamp, till the main body of the army is put in motion.

I was much pleafed at a little politeffe and attention of that amiable woman, Lady Harriet Ackland---Exclufive of the excellent qualities that had already endeared her to the officers of the grenadiers (which corps Major Ackland commands) fhe thought proper to exprefs a fenfe of their attention to her (and who could be inattentive?) by fome little prefent; fo a few days before the officers took the field, fhe fent each of them, (thirty in number) half of a large Chefhire cheefe, which was no fuch fmall prefent as you may imagine, Englifh cheefe being then a dollar per pound; and perhaps it may not occur to you, there is no prefent you can fend to an

European

European abroad, fo great as good Chefhire cheefe. If you fhould be inclined to fend me one, and this is no fmall hint, let me defire you to enclofe it in lead, and then in horfe-hair, the former to preferve the moifture, and the latter as the only fafe-guard againft the amazing large rats that are in fuch great abundance in almoft all fhips.

It much pleafed me to obferve the manner in which the inhabitants kept Holy Thurf-day, which they term *La Fête Dieu.* On the evening preceding that day, I could not conceive the reafon that the people were bringing cart loads of fmall firs into the city; but judge how great was my fur-prize in the morning, when I went to the parade, to find the ftreets fwept as clean as poffible, thefe trees ftuck in the ground on each fide, and fo contrived that their tops united, that every ftreet had the appearance of a grove, and upon enquiry found

it

was intended for the celebration of this great feftival.

About eleven o'clock the proceffion began from the great Church, which extended near half a mile in length. All the principal Clergy, the Friars of the different Convents, with a large band of mufic attending; in the center of the proceffion, under a canopy of crimfon velvet, fupported by fix Priefts, the High Prieft carried the HOST, upon a Bible, covered with a white napkin, and before him two men bore a large bafket full of flowers, which were ftrewed by feveral little boys in furplices; four others, with filver chalices, were continually wafting the incenfe towards the Hoft, the people at the fame time finging anthems. In this manner the proceffion went through moft of the ftreets in the city, and thofe who met it fell inftantly on their knees; thofe who remained in their houfes, came to the windows

and

and did the fame. I cannot but fay it was a pleafing fight, and could not help thinking but it muft be magnificent indeed, in thofe countries where the Roman Catholic is the eftablifhed religion.

We were apprized of fome proceffion, from an order given the day preceding by General Phillips, but had no idea of feeing fuch a fpectacle. There having been feveral difputes in Roman Catholic countries, concerning the refpect that the military fhould pay the Hoft, when paffing by, his Majefty, a few years ago, iffued out a general order for that purpofe, which General Phillips gave out in orders as follows :—
" As to-morrow there will be a great pro-
" ceffion through the city, I need not in-
" form the officers of the refpect and
" attention his Majefty has required fhould
" be paid the Hoft, when paffing. The
" non-commiffioned officers are defired to
" be particular in informing the men, that

Vol. I.   P   " when

" when the Hoft is going by, they are to
" front it, and behave in a decent and re-
" spectful manner, to pull off their hats,
" and remain in that fituation till the pro-
" ceffion has paffed. Any complaint that
" is made to the General, will be punifhed
" with the utmoft feverity."

To-morrow I leave this city, to join the advanced corps at the river *La Cole*. Situated as I muft be, confined to the company, which I am proud in faying is commanded by Lord Peterfham, you cannot expect the whole detail of the manœuvres of the different actions that may happen, or a particular account of the fiege of Ticonderoga. I fhall however inform you of every thing that comes under my own obfervation, and give you my opinion of events, not as an officer, but merely as a fpectator.

The officers take the field under great disadvantages, in regard to horses to transport their baggage, when they quit the Lakes; those for the use of Government are sent through the woods to Crown Point, but their arrival at that place is very uncertain, as they are liable to be taken by the enemy. It is quite a hazard, but rather than be distressed when I get to Ticonderoga, I have risqued sending mine, with some others, through the woods; if they arrive safe it will be a vast convenience; if not, I shall be compelled to send back my baggage, and then, hey for courage and a knapsack!

Should any misfortune attend the cattle intended for Government, it will greatly retard the army, provided the Americans should abandon Ticonderoga; at all events it will impede us in some measure, as it will be several days after the army gets there before the horses arrive, and you may eafily conceive an army cannot move without its artillery and provifions.

Another great difadvantage which we experience in the profecution of this war, and which the Americans avoid is, that we have to tranfport all our provifions with us, whereas they have magazines ftored with great abundance, every thirty or forty miles; where, in cafe any difafter attends their army, the lofs of their provifions is eafily recruited. But if any fuch event fhould happen with us, we fhould be obliged to make a ftand at fome ftrong poft, till provifions could be fent from Canada.

Added to this, the Americans are by much our fuperiors at wood-fighting, being habituated to the woods from their infancy. Our fuccefs in any engagement muft greatly reft on the bayonet, the great utility of which General Burgoyne pointed out in an order a few days fince, ftrongly recom-

recommending the officers to inculcate that idea into the minds of the men.

After I leave this city, you muft not expect to hear from me fo regularly as you have lately. But you may reft affured, I fhall embrace every opportunity of letting you know I am not yet food for the crows.

Yours, &c.

LETTER XIX.

Montreal, May 26th, 1777.

MY DEAR FRIEND,

A FEW days since I was invited to dine with Capt. Frazer, who is superintendant over the Indians, and who gave us a dinner entirely of wild-meats. Most of the dishes were only to set off the table, there being such things there as very few of the company could partake of; we had the leg of a bear, indeed, which was salted, and far exceeded in flavor a leg of pork; another dish, which though deemed a great rarity with you, is not esteemed such here, a very fine haunch of venison.

To

To tell you the truth, I really made my repaſt of what *Monſieur Roberdeau*, of Quebec, hinted to me, of the *Friandiſes*.

Juſt as the cloth was removed, there came into the room a great number of Indians, (and amongſt them one very old) who not having much ceremony, and ſeeing the bottles and glaſſes on the table, would drink with us, and began to be extremely troubleſome, when Capt. Frazer interfered, and to ſhew you the controul he has over them, the inſtant he ſpoke, they quitted the room, but not without a preſent, for I did not underſtand the Indian language, but as I thought, and as he afterwards told us he was obliged to order his ſervant to give them a bottle of rum.

After we had got rid of theſe troubleſome gueſts, and the table reſtored to order, Capt. Frazer ſaid, Gentlemen, I obſerved you all took notice of that old Indian, which

which the company acquiefcing in, he told the following very fingular hiftory relative to him:

That Indian, faid he, is of the *Algonquin* nation, who are converted to Chriftianity, and who, being attached to the French, had excited the enmity of the *Iroquois*, whofe hatred to Chriftians carried them to every excefs of fury, murdering and tormenting to death, without any regard to fex or age, every one that had the misfortune to fall into their hands. To efcape the fury of the *Iroquois*, the whole nation of the *Algonquins* were determined to fight their way to the French, in which ftruggle the women took no inconfiderable fhare, but nobly refifted their enemies on this occafion, when it fo happened, that the mother of that old Indian was taken prifoner.

The *Iroquois* carried her to one of their villages, ftripped her naked, bound her hand

hand and foot in one of their cabins, and in that ſtate ſhe remained for ten days, the ſavages ſleeping round every night. The 11th night, when they were all aſleep, ſhe diſengaged herſelf from the ropes they had bound her with and fled into the foreſt. The ſecond day after her eſcape, her footſteps were perceived by the *Iroquois* who were in ſearch of her, and they purſued her with ſuch expedition, that the third day ſhe diſcovered them cloſe at her heels: ſhe inſtantly plunged into a pond of water that was near her, and diving amongſt ſome weeds and bulruſhes, juſt kept her head above water, ſo as to breathe, and by this ſtratagem eſcaped from her purſuers, who, after making a moſt diligent ſearch, went away the courſe they thought ſhe would take. When night came on, ſhe left her ſituation, and took a different route to that ſhe perceived the ſavages had taken, by which means this poor creature wandered through the woods for five and
thirty

thirty days, without any other fuftenance than roots and wild-berries. At length fhe came to the river St. Laurence, and not perceiving any canoe along the fhore, made a kind of wicker raft, on which fhe croffed the river, and had paffed by Montreal, not knowing well in what part of the river fhe was, when, perceiving a canoe full of favages, and fearful left they might be *Iroquois*, fhe again ran into the woods, and remained till fun-fet, when fhe directed her courfe to Montreal.--- Within a mile of the city, fhe was difcovered by a party whom fhe knew to be *Algonquins*; when they approached her, fhe fquatted down behind a bufh, calling out to them that fhe was not in a condition to be feen, as fhe was naked; one of them then threw her a blanket, and conducted her into the fort. After Capt. Frazer had related this ftory, he told us this old Indian took great pleafure in telling it to every one, at the fame time expreffing the utmoft

utmoft indignation, and vowing revenge againft the *Iroquois*.

We had fcarcely drank five glaffes, after Captain Frazer had finifhed his narration, when the Indians returned, upon a pretence of bufinefs to him, which was no other than that of procuring more rum, which Captain Frazer refufing them, they grew extremely troublefome, and what, with the liquor they had already drank, were much beyond any controul, for they paid no attention to Capt. Frazer, who, finding he could not pacify, or any way get rid of them, made us an apology, and the company broke up.

On my return home, mentioning to my landlord what I had heard concerning the *Iroquois*, he faid, *Monfieur, les Iroquois font le plus fauvage et frauduleux de tout*, and related the fad cataftrophe of a Miffionary, one *Father Jogues*, who refided a little below

low *Trois Rivieres*: imagining he had made great progress in converting them to Christianity, during a short interval of peace, was willing to spread his doctrine amongst the remote of the *Iroquois*; for that purpose, he set out with four Indians, and a young Frenchman as his servant; he had not passed *Trois Rivieres* above a league, when his four savage guides abandoned them: yet such was his enthusiasm and confidence of having wrought upon them so far, that his person was in safety, he would not return, but travelled on, and at the very first *Iroquois* village he and his servant came to, he was too fatally convinced of his error, for they were seized, stript, scourged, buffeted, and treated as prisoners of war. At this sudden change the good Father was in great amazement, and began (for he could speak their language) to expostulate with all the powers of elocution, which were of no avail, and the only favor that his eloquence could

procure

procure him was, that inſtead of burning him and his companion alive, they humanely condeſcended to behead them with a hatchet. After my landlord had finiſhed the ſtory, he ſaid, with great warmth and indignation, *Monſieur, les Iroquois ſont frauduleux comme le Diable, et en voyagent j'ai toujours crainte de le rencontre;* and, from the ſtory he had related, you will no doubt ſay he had very good foundation for his fears.

I am, yours, &c.

LETTER XX.

Montreal, May 31*ſt*, 1777.

MY DEAR FRIEND,

BEFORE I leave this city, though there is not much leiſure time on my hands, I ſhall communicate to you the fruit of my enquiries (to which I have applied myſelf this winter) reſpecting the advantage England derives from Canada.

It was a complaint, and perhaps not without foundation, that Canada never enriched France, and that none of its inhabitants acquired the leaſt fortunes, but the Indian traders. As it was not the fault

fault of the country, which has many staple commodities, from which a source of wealth might be derived, whence then is to be attributed this cause? First, from the continual state of warfare this province has been in from its very first settlement; to the oppressiveness of the government, and the rapaciousness of the clergy; from which causes (except those enterprizing people who embark in the fur trade) the inhabitants not having a stimulative motive, were content with a mere existence, and if a Canadian could but pay his tythes and duties to his priest, and lay up a little to enjoy a long tedious winter, his happiness was compleat.

But the scene is now reversed; all over the province there are saw and grist-mills, and the Canadians are now enriching themselves, by exporting lumber and grain to the West Indies and the other provinces. As I observed before, it was not the fault of of the country, for to perfons induftrioufly inclined, this country has many advantages, as after they have tilled their ground in autumn, from that time till the middle of April and the begining of May, when they fow their crops, they have to cut down timber, and to faw it for building, fhipping, and other ufes, ready for exportation when the froft breaks up. Another great advantage this country poffeffes, is the quick vegetation, for the crop that is fown in May fprings up, grows to perfection, is cut down and carried into the barns by the end of Auguft.

Without confidering the hardfhips and difficulties they were expofed to, the Indian trader was always looked upon with an envious eye: but now, as they are not liable to the rapacity of ftate and clergy, but enjoy all the privileges of our happy conftitution, their induftry is very great, and thofe winters that ufed to be fpent in feafting feasting and pleasure, is now employed to more useful purposes, and an Indian trader is not now a man so much to be envied.

Daily experience shews, that this province is capable of producing more resources than one. What motives of policy could it be in the French to keep the Canadians in such a state of oppression? It should seem that France was sufficiently proud in having this vast territory annexed to its crown, and content with the produce of the fur trade. But lest you think I am entering too deeply into politics, I shall conclude, deferring to my next an account of the fur trade, which still is the greatest resource of wealth to England, but which must in process of time be annihilated, from the very great destruction of the animals, which every year diminishes them so fast, and occasions their flying to remoter parts, that the trader has hundreds of leagues farther to go in search of them; the necessity, therefore of encouraging husbandry, will appear evident to you. But I see I am again running into politics, therefore adieu.

Yours, &c.

LETTER XXI.

Montreal, June 3d, 1777.

MY DEAR FRIEND,

I NOW proceed to give you some account of the fur trade, and as in one of my former letters the nature of Indian traders were described to you and their modes of trafficking with the savages, I shall give you some little account of the beasts, whose furs they go in search of, and hope you will not think any little remarks that I may intersperse, as dictating to your superior sense and understanding, but merely ideas that occur to me whilst writing.

By the accounts moſt authors have given us of Canada, they deſcribe it, upon its firſt diſcovery, to have been an immenſe tract of foreſt, ſerving only as an extenſive haunt to wild beaſts, with which it was over-run, and which had multiplied prodigiouſly; for thoſe few men who did inhabit thoſe deſerts, not having any flocks or tame animals, left more room and food for thoſe that were wandering and free, like themſelves; and although there was no great variety, ſtill there were multitudes of each ſpecies. But they, as every thing, ſooner or later, in this terreſtrial globe, paid tribute to the ſovereignty of man; that cruel power that has been ſo fatal to every living creature, and the few that the natives deſtroyed for their food and cloathing, were of little note in ſuch a prodigious multitude. No ſooner had our luxury led us to make uſe of their ſkins, than the natives waged a perpetual war againſt them, which they carried on with great eagerneſs, as in

return

return for the havoc and destruction they made amongst them, they indulged in a plenty and variety of gratifications they were before unaccustomed to; and to render the war the more destructive, we assisted them with fire-arms, by the means of which great quantities of furs, and of a prodigious variety, were procured. Most of these were known in Europe, which were the same as those that came from the northern parts of our hemisphere, but they were in too small quantities to supply a great demand.

Caprice and novelty has made these furs more or less in fashion, and England has found it to be for the interest of Canada, that they should be valued at home; and that they are so with a witness, the enormous price your sister gave for a muff and tippet, is a convincing proof: here I assure you they are very dear, the commonest fur cap standing you in two guineas.

Having given you a little hiftory of furs, I fhall now defcribe to you fome of the beafts whofe fkins are ftill in requeft, and firft begin with the Otter, which is fo generally known in England, as to need no defcription; there is no other difference than that it is much larger, and its hair blacker and finer than ours, a circumftance fatal to them, as expofing them more to the purfuit of the favages.

The Pole-cat, of which there are three fpecies, is in great eftimation among the Canadian hunters, as the hair is darker, more gloffy, and more filky than thofe in Europe.

Even the Rat of North-America is valuable for its fkin; but the two principal ones that are in the article of trade is the Oppoffum and the Mufk; many and ridiculous are the ftories which are propagated relative to the female of the former, fuch

as,

among othrs, that of the young ones getting into the belly again through the teats, the fact is this, under its belly there is a loose skin, with a small aperture in the center, and this she can expand or depress at will; if pursued, and she thinks her young are in danger, she puts them into this bag, and runs away with them up a tree. Another singular instance of sagacity in this animal, which is seldom mentioned, is, that if pursued by other animals, such as the Tiger, Mountain-cat, &c. that can mount trees, it goes to the extremity of a bough, and suspends itself by its tail. The skin of the Musk-rat is employed for the same purposes as the Beaver, of which he seems to be a diminutive; but its most intrinsic value is for that predominant and powerful perfume it produces, and which is called after this animal.

The Ermine is about the size of a squirrel, but not so long, has the same lively eyes,

keen

look, and his motions are so quick, that the eye can scarcely follow them, it has a long bushy tail, which at the tip is as black as jet; what enables me to give you so exact a description of this little animal is, that the daughter of the gentleman at whose house I lodge, has one in her possession; indeed it is the fashion for the young ladies to keep them, as ours do squirrels. One thing not a little extraordinary of this animal is, that all the winter it was white as snow, and the other day, when admiring it, I expressed a surprize in perceiving it had a yellow tint, when the young lady said, *Ah! Monsieur, au milieu de l'été c'est jaune comme d'or.* This little animal is reckoned one of the beauties of Canada, for though the sable is smaller, it is not so common.

The Martin, whose skin is the most valuable, is only to be met with in the center of the forests, far from any habitation, and

and although fo fmall an animal, is a beaft
of prey, living entirely upon birds. It is
but a foot and a half long, yet leaves a
print in the fnow, which appears to be
the footftep of a larger animal, occafioned
by its jumping along and giving the marks
of both feet together: their fur is much
efteemed, but is inferior to that fpecies
which are called fables, whofe fkins are
of a fhining black. Thofe of the Martin
encreafe in value from the various dyes,
the deeper the tint the more valuable, and
they gradually encreafe from a light brown
to the deep gloffy black of the fable. The
Martins feldom more than once in two or
three years quit their receffes in thefe im-
penetrable woods, and when they do, the
Canadians take it as a fign of a good winter, imagining there will be great quantities of fnow, and confequently good fport
in deftroying them.

The

The Wild-cat of Canada is reckoned much fmaller than thofe upon the northern continent of Europe, and is the fame kind of animal that was called by the ancients the Lynx, of which an erroneous opinion has ever prevailed amongft the vulgar, that it is poffeffed of the power of piercing to death with its eyes whatever it deftines for its prey, as nature had deprived it of the faculties of hearing and fmelling at a diftance, which miftaken notion muft have arifen from this fimple caufe, that as this animal lives upon what game it can catch, it will purfue it to the very tops of the talleft trees, and nature having endowed it with a quicker fight than moft other animals, whatever it purfues, though of ever fo fmall a nature, it never lofes fight of, let the foliage of the trees be ever fo thick. The flefh of this animal is very white, and faid to be well flavored, but the Indians hunt it chiefly for its fkin, the hair of it being long, and of a fine light
grey,

grey, but not so valuable as that of the fox.

This animal, like other natives of the frozen climates, where nature produces but few vegetables, is carniverous.

Besides the small furs, Canada supplies England with the skins of the Stag, Deer, Roebuck, the Caribou and the Elk, the latter of which is supposed to be the original of all these species. All these animals are hunted by the Canadians, but the chace of the Bear the savages have reserved to themselves, and which is their favorite sport; it seems best adapted to their warlike manners, strength and bravery, and especially as those animals supply most of their wants.

Fearful left you may grow tired of this heavy detail of wild beasts, I shall conclude this, reserving to my next the description of of the only two that are worthy of notice, the Bear and the Beaver, the latter of which poffeffes all the friendly difpofitions, divefted of all the vices and misfortunes that await us, and which debars us from the true and real pleafures arifing from the friendly and fweet intercourfe that fhould fubfift between man and man.

Yours, &c.

LETTER XXII.

Montreal, June 7th, 1777.

MY DEAR FRIEND,

OPPORTUNITIES almoſt daily occuring, I am happy to embrace them, during the little time I have to remain in this city; when I quit it, you will think me very remifs in addreſſing you. Let me ſincerely aſſure you, although there will be no regular conveyance, I ſhall embrace every opportunity that offers.

As in my laſt I mentioned to you that the ſavages were ſupplied with moſt of their wants from the Bear, feeding upon
its

its flefh, rubbing themfelves with its greafe, and cloathing themfelves with its fkin, it may not be amifs to give you fome little account of this animal, and the fingular method they have of deftroying them.

As no doubt you muft have feen many of them in England, I fhall only give you an account of fome of its particularities.

This animal is rather fhy than fierce, and will feldom attack a man; on the contrary, they will fly at the fight of him, and a dog will drive them a great way. The only time they are dangerous is after having been wounded, when they quit the hollow trees they have refided in all the winter, and at the time of rutting, which is in the month of July; they are then fo fierce and ill-tempered, the effects of jealoufy, that they are extremely dangerous to meet with. At this feafon they grow very lean, and their flefh has fo difagreeable a relifh, that the Indians, whofe

whofe ftomachs are none of the moft delicate, will not touch it. Who could conceive that an animal, fo unlovely in its appearance, fhould in the fpace of one month grow leaner by the *belle paffion*, than after an abftinence of fix months.

But the feafon over, he recovers his former *embonpoint*, which he is greatly affifted in regaining by the great quantity of fruits the woods abound with, and of which he is extremely greedy; grapes he is particularly fond of, climbing after them up the moft lofty trees. After he has fed for fome time on fruits, his flefh becomes delicious, and continues fo till fpring.

It is furprizing enough that this animal, although provided with fo warm a fur, and not of the moft delicate appearance, fhould take more precautions than any other to preferve itfelf from the cold, (this may ferve as a leffon from nature,

not

not to form our judgment of things by appearance, fince every one is the beft judge of his own wants;) for which purpofe, when the winter fets in, he climbs up the hollow rotten trunk of an old tree, ftopping up the entrance with pine branches, by which means he is fheltered from all inclemencies of the weather, and when once lodged, he feldom or ever quits his apartment during the winter, which is the more fingular, it being certain that he lays up no manner of provifion, and that he muft require fome nourifhment. That he requires little food is natural to fuppofe, as at the end of autumn he is very fat, takes no exercife, and almoft always fleeps, and, therefore, lofing little by perfpiration, has very feldom occafion to go abroad in queft of it, and when he does, haftens back to his retreat. A ridiculous notion is gone abroad into the world, that during the winter the fole nourifhment of the Bear is licking its paws, which, no' doubt, arofe

from

from the amazing long time thefe animals can, either through the nourifhment they receive from fleep, or idlenefs, go without food. Yet that fuch an idea fhould prevail, I am not furprized, as there has been an inftance of one that was chained for a whole winter without either food or drink, and at the end of fix months was found as fat as when firft caught.

The feafon for hunting the bear is in winter, when the Indians force him from his habitation by fetting fire to the pine branches that he has drawn together at the bottom of the hollow tree, when the fmoke afcending up the trunk, drives him from his late comfortable habitation, from which he no fooner defcends, than they kill him. The Indians now only deftroy them to anfwer their own wants, as formerly they ufed to do for the purpofe of difpofing of their fkins to the traders; but it was no fooner underftood that

Canada was ſtored with Beavers, than the ſavages, urged on by a more lucrative intereſt, directed their war againſt an animal the moſt harmleſs, who moleſts no living creature, and is neither carniverous nor ſanguinary. This is, I am ſorry to obſerve, become an object of man's moſt earneſt purſuit, and the one that the ſavages hunt after with the greateſt eagerneſs and cruelty; a circumſtance entirely owing to the unmerciful rapaciouſneſs which luxury has made neceſſary in ſkins, for all the poliſhed nations of Europe.

This animal is by nature adapted for ſocial life, being endowed with an inſtinct in the preſervation and propagation of its ſpecies; it is generally about three or four feet long, moſtly weighing from forty to ſixty pounds; the hinder feet are webbed, which enables it to ſwim, and in the fore feet the toes are divided; its tail is oval, very flat, and covered with ſcales; the head

reſembles

resembles that of a rat, in which are four very sharp teeth, with these it will gnaw through trees of a great circumference.

This animal is divested of turbulent passions, without a desire of doing injury to any one, free from craft, scarcely defending itself, unless it lives in society; it never bites, except when caught, and as nature has not supplied it with any weapons of defence, by a natural instinct as it were, it forms societies, and has various contrivances to secure its ease, without fighting, and to live without committing, or suffering an injury; although this peaceable, and you may say almost tame animal, enters into society, it is nevertheless independent, every want being supplied by itself, and therefore it is a slave to none. It will not serve, nor does it pretend to command, every care seems directed by an instinct, that at the same time, as it labors for the general good, it lives for itself alone.

alone. To learn the nature of the focieties of thefe animals, as it was related to me by my landlord, may afford you the fame entertainment it did me.

In the month of June or July, they affemble from all quarters, to the number of two or three hundred, near fome lake or pool of water, to build their habitations againft winter, the conftruction of which, from the complication and manner of difpofing the materials, one would be led to imagine to be beyond the capacity of any one but an intelligent being, and efpecially in their conftructing of dams, when they cannot meet with a lake or pool; in this cafe they fix upon fome river, when the firft of their labour is to make a dam, which they generally do in the fhalloweft part of the ftream, for that purpofe felling trees with the four fharp teeth that I have already defcribed; five or fix of them will gnaw a large

one

one through, and to mark to you the wonderful fagacity of thefe induftrious brutes, they contrive it fo that it always falls in the water: having laid this foundation, they fell fmaller trees, which they roll to this great one, but what appears the moft wonderful is, the manner they fink the piles in the water, to prevent the ftream's carrying away the trees, they lay acrofs. Their contrivance is this, with their nails they dig a hole in the ground, or at the bottom of the water, with their teeth they reft the ftake againft the bank of the river, or againft the tree that lies acrofs, and with their feet they raife the ftake and fink it with the fharp end (which thefe fenfible animals make to it) in the hole that they have made, where it ftands up; and to render thefe ftakes or piles more fecure, they interweave branches of fmall trees, and with their tails wilk up a kind of mortar with clay, and fill the vacant fpace of the interwoven branches.

After

After this work is finifhed by the body at large, each one confiders of fome lodging for himfelf; an hut being built upon piles on the fides of the Lake, capable of containing from two or three to ten or fifteen, (for they divide themfelves into companies, and build thefe huts accordingly;) which are formed with walls and partitions of about two feet thick and as many in height, arched over, and the whole fo plaiftered with clay, that the fmalleft breath of air cannot penetrate through them; each apartment is made large enough to contain two, a male and female; each hut has two entrances, one towards the land, and the other on the fide towards the ftream, the former for them to go into the woods to fetch provifions, and the latter to efcape from their enemy, that is to fay MAN, the deftroyer of cities and commonwealths. The infide of their apartments has no other furniture than the flooring of grafs covered with

the

the boughs of the fir, and thefe animals are fo cleanly, that no filth of any kind is ever feen in thefe apartments.

In each hut there are ftore houfes proportionate to the number of its inhabitants; every one knows its own, and never fteals from his neighbour. Each party, that is to fay, the male and female, live in their own habitations; they have no jealoufies or quarrels; the provifions of the community are collected and expended without any conteft, and reft fatisfied with the fimple food that their labors procure them. The only paffion they have is that of conjugal affection, wherein a moft excellent example is held forth to that all-wife and all-fufficient man, who is led away by every guft of paffion and vanity.

Two of thefe animals, in the courfe of their labours in the fummer months, match together, unite by inclination and reciprocal

ciprocal choice, and agree to pafs the winter, and like too many couple who haftily enter into matrimony with equally as good motives, but forgetting what fhould make the happinefs lafting, that of laying up a ftock to guard againft an inclement feafon.

The happy couple retire to their hut about the end of autumn, which has been obferved to be no lefs favorable to love than fpring; for if the feafon of flowers invites the feathered tribe to propagate in the woods, the feafon of fruits as powerfully excites the inhabitants of the earth in the reproduction of their fpecies; befides, as winter gives leifure for amorous purfuits, it compenfates for the advantages of other feafons.

I am this moment told that the pacquet is going to fail, and muft therefore defer a further account of this wonderful and
furprizing

surprizing animal, from whom so many lessons of industry and morality may be drawn, till another opportunity, and conclude with assuring you of my best wishes for your happiness and prosperity, and that I remain

Yours, &c.

LETTER XXIII.

Montreal, June 8th, 1777.

MY DEAR FRIEND,

I SEND this by our friend Captain F. who is going poft to Quebec, from which place he will fail immediately, and as the navigation from this city to Quebec is much delayed by the various currents and other caufes in the river, he will be there as foon, if not fooner, than the fhip I fent my firft by, in which cafe you may receive this before the other, which may greatly bewilder you. I therefore fhall juft hint to you, this is the conclufion of the hiftory of the Beaver.

If

If my recollection does not deceive me, I left off in my laſt at deſcribing his love, that univerſal paſſion of nature, which the Beaver ſeems to enjoy in the conjugal ſtate, comparatively much happier than mankind; for when they couple and enter their huts, they never quit each other, conſecrating their whole time to love, from which neither labor nor any other object can divert them.

If by chance a ſun-ſhiny day ſhould happen to enliven the gloomy melancholy of the ſeaſon, the happy couple leave their huts to walk on the borders of the Lake, regaling themſelves with ſome freſh bark, and breathing the ſalutary exhalations of the earth. At the concluſion of the winter, the mother brings forth the endearing pledges of their affection, while the father ranges the woods, allured by the ſweets of the ſpring, leaving to his little family that portion of room which he took up in

his

his narrow cell. The Beaver generally produces two or three, which the mother fuckles, nurfes and trains up, for when the father is abfent, fhe takes out the young ones, in her excurfions for cray and other fifh, and green bark to recruit her own ftrength and to feed her young, till the feafon of labor returns; for although thefe animals are fo induftrious as to build themfelves habitations that would laft them a century, they are obliged to rebuild them every year, as the firft thing the traders do when they meet with any of their works, is to break down their cabins and the dam, together with their dyke.

There are various methods of taking and deftroying thefe animals, by draining the water from their dykes, and fometimes by fnares; they are very feldom fhot at, for unlefs killed on the fpot, they are loft to the huntfman, by plunging into the water wounded, when they fink to the bottom
and

and never rife. The moft certain and general mode of catching them is by fetting traps in the woods, where they perceive them to have been eating the bark of the young trees; they bait thefe traps with frefh flips of wood, which the Beaver no fooner touches, than a great weight falls and crufhes its loins, when the huntfman, who lies concealed near the fpot, haftens to kill it.

No doubt but by this time you are heartily tired with fo long a detail of this animal; but if I have deviated from the common path of defcription, I can only fay it has proceeded from thefe two caufes, that I cannot fufficiently admire the many virtues it poffeffes, divefted of all manner of vice, and have been loft in the contemplation of that Divine Being, who formed it with all thefe natural endowments.

You muſt pardon my making a compariſon between the focieties of theſe animals and thoſe of a convent. If happineſs may be ſaid to dwell in both communities, it muſt be allowed to be by very oppoſite means. The happineſs of one conſiſts in following the dictates of nature; in the other, nature, the ſweets of ſocial love, and the laws of our creation, are totally deſtroyed! The inſtitution of the ſociety of the Beaver, ſeems ſolely to propagate its ſpecies; the other to annihilate it. How many, who might have dignified nature under the character of a fond mother and an affectionate wife, are loſt to the world and to themſelves!---they cannot help feeling tender emotions, and, in the bitterneſs of miſery, execrate that tyrant cuſtom, which has torn them from the embraces of happineſs and chained them in cells, a prey to affections hopeleſs and inſatiable---the idea carries me beyond myſelf.

What

What will not the feelings of humanity exclaim, when it confiders that thefe gloomy and ferocious inftitutions are wafting away in all parts of Europe! Inftitutions not only injurious but inhuman, which, under the abfurd and ridiculous notion of making men equal to angels, robs health of its vigor, and beauty of its reward.

I am moft agreeably interrupted in my ferious reflections, by a vifit from our friend S——, who is juft arrived from New-York; he was taken prifoner in the courfe of laft fummer, by a notorious fellow of the name of Whitcomb, the fame man who fhot Brigadier General Gordon, the particulars of which I fhall inform you in my next.

Yours, &c.

LETTER XXIV.

Montreal, June 12*th,* 1777.

MY DEAR FRIEND,

IN my laft I mentioned to you the name of one Whitcomb, a native of Connecticut, and a great partizan of the Americans, who, after the defeat upon the Lakes, offered his fervice to venture through the woods, and bring in prifoner an Englifh officer, for which purpofe he ftationed himfelf among the thickeft copfes that are between *La Prairé* and St. John's. The firft officer who happened to pafs him was Brigadier General Gordon; he was mounted on a fpirited horfe, and Whitcomb thinking

thinking there was little probability of feizing him, fired at and wounded him in the fhoulder. The General immediately rode as faft as he could to the camp at St. John's, which he had but juft reached, when with lofs of blood and fatigue, he fell from his horfe; fome foldiers, took him up and carried him to the hofpital, where, after his wound was dreffed, and he was a little at eafe, he related the circumftance, which being immediately made known to General Carleton, a party of Indians were fent out to fcour the woods, and fearch for Whitcomb, but in vain, as he haftened back to Ticonderoga. General Carleton, however, imagining he might be lurking about the woods, or fecreted in the houfe of fome difaffected Canadian, iffued out a proclamation among the inhabitants, offering a reward of fifty guineas to any one that would bring Whitcomb, alive or dead, to the camp.

A few days after this General Gordon died of his wound, in whose death we sincerely lamented the loss of a brave and experienced officer.

When Whitcomb returned to Ticonderoga, and informed the General who commanded there, that although he could not take an officer prisoner, he believed he had mortally wounded one, the General expressed his disapprobation in the highest terms, and was so much displeased at the transaction, that Whitcomb, in order to effect a reconciliation, offered his service to go again, professing he would forfeit his life, if he did not return with a prisoner.

He accordingly, with two other men, proceeded down Lake *Champlain*, in a canoe, to a small creek, where they secreted it, and repaired to the woods, to the same spot where Whitcomb had stationed himself before; the two men lay concealed a little way

way in the wood, whilſt he ſkulked about the borders of it.

The regiment of which our friend S——
is Quarter-maſter, having occaſion for ſome ſtores from Montreal, he was going from the campt at St. John's to procure them; he was adviſed not to go this road, but by way of *Chamblée*, on account of the late accident, but you know him to be a man of great bravery and perſonal courage, joined with uncommon ſtrength; reſolving not to go ſo many miles out of his road for any Whitcomb whatever, he jocoſely added, that he ſhould be very glad to meet with him, as he was ſure he ſhould get the reward; in this, however, he was greatly miſtaken, his reward being noother than that of being taken priſoner himſelf.

Previous to his ſetting out he took every precaution, having not only loaded his fuſée, but charged a brace of piſtols; when
he

he came near to the woods I have already scribed, he was very cautious, but in an inftant, Whitcomb and the two men he had with him fprung from behind a thick bufh, and feized him before he could make the leaft refiftance; they then took from him his fufée and piftols, tied his arms behind him with ropes, and blind-folded him.

It was three days before they reached the canoe that had been concealed, during which time they had but very fcanty fare; a few hard bifcuits ferved to allay hunger, while the fruit of the woods was a luxury!--- When Whitcomb had marched him to fuch a diftance as he thought he could not make his efcape, were he at liberty, through fear of lofing himfelf, for the greater eafe on his own part, and to facilitate their march, they untied his hands, and took the cloth from his eyes. Only picture to yourfelf what muft have been his feelings, at feeing himfelf in the midft of a thick wood, furrounded

rounded by three defperate fellows, and uncertain as to their intentions!

At night, when they had partaken of their fcanty pittance, two out of the three ufed to fleep, whilft the other kept watch. The firft night he flept through fatigue; on the fecond, as you may naturally fuppofe, from his great anxiety of mind, he could not clofe his eyes, in the middle of which an opportunity occurred whereby he could have effected his efcape, for the man whofe watch it was, fell faft afleep. He has fince told me how his mind wavered for a length of time, what meafures to purfue; he could not bear the idea of putting them to death, though juftified by the rules of war: if he efcaped from them, they might in all probability retake and ill-treat him. The great hazard of all, which determined him to abide by his fate was, that by being fo many miles in a tract of wood, where he could not tell what

direction

direction to take (having been blind-folded when he entered it) he might poffibly wander up and down till he perifhed with hunger. In this reftlefs ftate, he remained till day-break, when they refumed their march, and in the evening came to the creek where the canoe was concealed ; they then fecured him again, put him in the canoe, and proceeded up the lake to Ticonderoga, where they arrived early the next morning. When they landed him he was again blind-folded, that he might not fee their works, and thus conducted to the General, whofe only motive for endeavouring to get an officer was, either by threats or intreaties, to gain information relative to our army. In this, however, he was greatly difappointed, and as he could not obtain the leaft intelligence from our friend, he ordered him as prifoner of war upon his parole, to fome of the interior towns, from which place, as I informed you in my laft, he is juft returned, as

hearty

hearty and well as ever. I fhould not have dwelt fo long on this fubject, but knowing you have his welfare fo much at heart, that you feel yourfelf interefted in whatever concerns him.

I fhall now conclude, but before I do fo, let me congratulate you on the recovery of your health, after fo alarming an illnefs. Good health alone fweetens life, and that you may long enjoy it, both for your own fake and that of your friends, is the ardent wifh of

Yours, &c.

LETTER XXV.

Camp at St. John's, June 14th, 1777.

MY DEAR FRIEND,

I HAD scarcely finished my last, when I received orders to march to this place, and am now entering upon the hurry and bustle of an active campaign. You must not accuse me now of inattention, if you should not hear from me so frequently.

As I observed in a former letter, it was the general opinion the King's troops would not be prevented passing Lake *Champlain*, but wait our arrival at Ticonderoga; in that case the operations of the campaign
will

will commence at Crown Point. It would be doing great injuſtice to thoſe who have been ſtationed at this garriſon during the winter, if I omitted to mention their great exertions in repairing, augmenting, and rendering fit for immediate ſervice the *batteaux*, gun-boats, and armed veſſels. The other parts of the army have been equally as induſtrious in eſtabliſhing magazines at Montreal, Sorell and *Chamblée*, which muſt be effected during the froſt, not only as the conveyance is eaſier at that time, but on account of the roads, which, by the running and melting of the ſnow, are generally impaſſable for ſome months.

By all the accounts that can be collected, the Americans are in great force at Ticonderoga, nearly to the amount of 12,000, and a conſiderable number occupy Lake George, ſuſtained by a great naval power, with a view, no doubt, of ſecuring their

retreat

in cafe they fhould be obliged to abandon Ticonderoga.

Should the navigation of Lake *Champlain* be fecured by the fuperiority of our naval force, the advanced corps, under the command of General Frafer, with a large body of favages and Canadians, for fcouts and out-works, and the beft of our engineers and artificers, are to take poffeffion of Crown Point, and to fortify it. The intention is with a view to prevent infult from the enemy, during the time neceffary for collecting ftores, forming magazines and fortifying pofts, all which muft be accomplifhed previous to our proceeding in force to lay fiege to Ticonderoga.

This brigade being ftationed at Crown Point, as a check on the enemy, the reft of the army are to be employed in forwarding the convoys and tranfports of provifions, removing artillery, preparing fafcines and other

other neceffaries for artillery operations, and to commence the fiege; and that the enemy during that period may not reft in tranquillity, corps of favages, fupported by detachments of the light infantry, are to keep them in continual alarm within their works, at the fame time to cover reconnoitering parties, both of general officers and engineers, and to obtain the beft intelligence of their ftrength, pofition and defign. From the great preparations that have been made during the winter, and by the vigorous exertion of the troops, who are in great health and fpirits, it may reafonably be expected that the reduction of Ticonderoga will be early in the fummer, unlefs fome misfortune, human prudence cannot forefee, fhould prevent it, although it is the general opinion it will be warmly contefted, and that there will be much blood-fhed. The Americans, when they drew the fword, muft have forefeen a bloody conteft, and expected all the horrors of a

war,

war, carried on as it were in their own bosoms, laying waste their fields of harvest, destroying every comfort, and introducing every misery mankind is capable of devising. But had certain persons, who were actuated by no other motives than a welfare and prosperity to both countries, directed their resolves, they would have advised a peaceable submission to the Mother Country, and easily prevented all the horrors of a civil war. America, from a number of aggregate fortunate circumstances, by slow degrees, had arisen to a state of great prosperity, and the power that she had fixed by that prosperity, bids fair to be of some duration, yet, in my opinion, not to such a degree as to establish her independence; her present distressed situation, without some other favorable circumstance, must inevitably prevent the execution of that idea. I am fully persuaded in my own mind, had they but reserved their ideas of independency for

half

half a century longer, from their increase of population and wealth, they would have fixed it without much difficulty, or even the assistance of any other power, and thus become the first nation in the world. In the present day, if they attain their boasted end, it must be by the arm of some nation, to whom, for want of resources to defray the expences of their alliance, she will be in continual broils and disputes, which may perhaps finally terminate in a total subjection, and that abject slavery they so ridiculously pretend to dread from us. Should this be the case, she will regret the loss of that protection from the Mother Country, she is now treating with so much ingratitude. Leaving you to your own remarks, for no doubt you will say, "a soldier and a politician!" I shall divert your attention from the cabals of mankind, to the wonderful productions of nature, in describing to you a little animal that was brought me lately, called a flying-squirrel.

This

This animal takes its name from being provided with a fkin, or membrane, which adheres to each fide, about the breadth of three inches, extending from its hind to fore feet, where it is connected by a bony articulation; it expands this membrane like a fail, by which it is enabled to fly from one tree to another, at a great diftance. Moft fquirrels will jump from tree to tree, when contiguous, but this animal will fly an incredible way. Its fkin is very foft, and of a beautiful dark grey, with eyes large, black, and very prominent; it fomewhat differs from the other fquirrels in its tafte, caring little for nuts, the chief and favorite food being the frefh tops of the birch. This little animal makes its bed in a very curious manner, of the mofs of the fame tree, in which it lies as it were buried, feldom ftirring from thence in the day time, unlefs difturbed. I came into poffeffion of it from a little drum-boy's going up a tree after a bird's neft, who

perceiving

perceiving it lay in that dormitory ſtate, ſeized it and brought it to me, for he had heard that I was making a collection of natural curioſities. By the bye, I beg you will inform me, in your next, if you received ſafe the little collection I ſent you from Montreal. I have added this curious animal, and one of another ſpecies, called the ground ſquirrel, which is a little larger than a mouſe, and moſt beautifully ſpotted like a fawn, to the collection I am now making, and hope they will be conſidered as tokens of friendſhip from

Yours, &c.

LETTER XXVI.

Camp at River Bouquet,
upon Lake Champlain, } *June* 23, 1777.

MY DEAR FRIEND,

WE have proceeded thus far, and, from all appearance, shall traverse the remainder of our way on the Lake, without meeting any opposition from the enemy, their design being, as I before mentioned to you, to dispute Ticonderoga; the intelligence from different spies and deserters fully confirm us in this opinion, who report, that they have labored hard to strengthen, and mean to dispute it most vigorously. They are now building row-gallies at Fort George, for the

defence

defence of that lake, and fortifying the road to Skenefborough.

It feems the Congrefs have configned to the four New England provinces, as they, are excellent axe-men, and very expeditious in felling of trees, the tafk of fupplying men and provifion to oppofe the progrefs of our forces, which they have undertaken, upon condition of being exempt from fupplying General Wafhington's army. If that really is the cafe, we fhall have bufinefs enough upon our hands, having four of the moft powerful and rebellious provinces to deal with; they have this advantage too, that upon their frontiers, fhould any difafter befall them, it can be fo eafily recruited, both as to men and provifions.

Having proceeded thus far up the lake, I am enabled to give you fome account of it, efpecially as we have paffed the broadeft part. There are many fmall iflands dif-
perfed

perfed in different parts, and where it is wideft, you are not able to difcern the oppofite' fhore; there are feveral plantations on each fide, but they are more numerous on the fouth, the north fide being lofty rocky mountains. It abounds with great quantities and variety of fifh; fturgeon, black bafs, mafquenongez, pike of an incredible fize, and many others, among which is a cat-fifh, which is about eighteen inches long, of a brownifh caft, without fcales, having a large round head, refembling that of a cat's, from which it derives its name; they have on their heads protuberances fimilar to the horns of a fnail, and like them can elevate and deprefs them at pleafure, and when fully extended, are about two inches long; if in liberating one of thefe fifh from the hook, it ftrikes you with one of its horns, it leaves an unaccountable and unpleafant fenfation on the part affected for two or three days. Its fins are very bony and

ftrong,

strong, like those of a perch, it commonly weighs about five or six pounds; the flesh is fat and luscious, greatly resembling the flavor of an eel.

There are at this season of the year prodigious flights of pigeons crossing the lake, of a most beautiful plumage, and in astonishing quantities.

These are most excellent eating, and that you may form some idea as to their number, at one of our encampments, the men for one day wholly subsisted on them; fatigued with their flight in crossing the lake, they alight upon the first branch they can reach to, many are so weary as to drop in the water, and are easily caught; those that alight upon a bough being unable to fly again, the soldiers knock down with long poles.

During the flights of thefe pigeons, which crofs this lake into Canada, and are continually flying about in large flocks, the Canadians find great amufement in fhooting them, which they do after a very fingular manner: in the day time they go into the woods, and make ladders by the fide of the tall pines, which the pigeons rooft on, and when it is dark they creep foftly under and fire up this ladder, killing them in great abundance; they then ftrike a light, and firing a knot of the pitch pine, pick up thofe they have killed, and the wounded ones that are unable to fly.— During the flights of thefe pigeons, which generally laft three weeks or a month, the lower fort of Canadians moftly fubfift on them

Now I am upon this fubject, it reminds me of what *Monfieur Blondeaux* was continually telling me of, *le grand plaifir que j'aurai quand l'été commencera en tuant les tourtes;*

tourtes; adding, at the same time, with great pleasure, *amusement que le Canadien aime beaucoup*. However, as to the numbers he used always to join with this observation, I generally thought my good landlord was setting off his country to great advantage by dealing in the marvellous, and should have been impressed with that idea, had I not been by ocular demonstration convinced to the contrary.

Not only at this encampment, but likewise at our former ones, we were under the necessity of clearing the thick underwood, and cutting down the small trees before we could encamp, during which time you are almost devoured with the musquitos, that swarm in great abundance, and are continually pestering you till the fires are lighted, when the smoke immediately disperses them.

In clearing the woods for our encampment at this place, a very favorite dog of Lord Balcarres's, of the Newfoundland breed, had a moſt miraculous eſcape; in the very inſtant that a heavy pine tree was falling, the dog run acroſs, the tree fell, and cruſhed the poor creature into the earth; in this ſituation every aſſiſtance was given, and when he was extricated, he came jumping and friſking up to his maſter, to the ſurprize of every one, who naturally imagined the creature muſt have had all its bones broken, for when the tree fell, it ſhook the earth ſome diſtance round. The preſervation of the dog is entirely attributed to the nature of the ſoil, which was ſandy and pliable. I need not, add, after this event, how much his Lordſhip prizes his favorite dog *Batteaux*.

Two miles up this river there is a ſawmill, and a fall of water, where there is moſt excellent trout-fiſhing. You who
are

are so fond of the diversion of angling, would find most excellent sport in this country. How I could wish you here, only for an hour, in that employment, that I might have the happiness, for that little time, of conversing with you, to ask you a thousand questions, to hear of those who are dear to me, to——but I must stop my reflection and my wishes together.

Yours, &c.

LETTER XXVII.

Camp at River Bouquet, upon Lake Champlain, } *June* 24, 17—.

MY DEAR FRIEND,

THIS river derives its name from a Colonel *Bouquet*, who commanded an expedition againſt the Indians, whilſt Canada was under the French Government, as at this place he had a converſation with them upon a treaty of peace.

It ſhould ſeem as if it was the deſtined ſpot to have intercourſe with Indians, for yeſterday General Burgoyne had a conference with them; and as I am ſenſible how much our employing Indians in this war

war is reprobated in England, I shall give you the General's speech, and their answer, of which you may form your own opinion. When the assembly were met, the General thus addressed them, by means of an interpreter:

" *Chiefs and Warriors*,

" The great King, our common father,
" and the patron of all who seek and de-
" serve his protection, has considered with
" satisfaction the general conduct of the
" Indian tribes, from the beginning of
" the troubles in America. Too sagacious
" and too faithful to be deluded or cor-
" rupted, they have observed the violated
" rights of the parental power they love,
" and burned to vindicate them. A few
" individuals alone, the refuse of a small
" tribe, at the first were led astray: and
" the misrepresentations, the specious al-
" lurements, the insidious promises, and
" diversified

" diverfified plots in which the rebels are
" exercifed, and all of which they employed
" for that effect, have ferved only in the
" end to enhance the honor of the tribes
" in general, by demonftrating to the
" world how few and how contemptible
" are the apoftates! It is a truth known
" to you all, thefe pitiful examples except-
" ed (and they have probably before this
" day hid their faces in fhame) the collec-
" tive voices and hands of the Indian tribes
" over this vaft continent, are on the fide
" of juftice, of law, and the King.

" The reftraint you have put upon your
" refentment in waiting the King your
" father's call to arms, the hardeft proof,
" I am perfuaded, to which your affection
" could have been put, is another mani-
" feft and affecting mark of your adher-
" ence to that principle of connection to
" which you were always fond to allude,
and

" and which is the mutual joy and the
" duty of the parent to cherish.

" The clemency of your father has been
" abused, the offers of his mercy have
" been despised, and his farther patience
" would, in his eyes, become culpable,
" in as much as it would with-hold re-
" dress from the most grievous oppressions
" in the provinces, that ever disgraced
" the history of mankind. It therefore
" remains for me, the General of one of
" his Majesty's armies, and in this council
" his representative, to release you from
" those bonds which your obedience im-
" posed—Warriors you are free—go forth
" in might and valor of your cause—strike
" at the common enemies of Great Britain
" and America—disturbers of public order,
" peace and happiness, destroyers of com-
" merce, parricides of state."

The

The General then directing their attentions, by pointing to the officers, both German and Britifh, that attended this meeting, proceeded:

" The circle round you, the chiefs of
" his Majefty's European forces, and of
" the Princes his allies, efteem you as
" brothers in the war; emulous in glory
" and in friendfhip, we will endeavor re-
" ciprocally to give and to receive ex-
" amples; we know how to value, and
" we will ftrive to imitate your prefever-
" ance in enterprize and your conftancy,
" to refift hunger, wearinefs and pain.
" Be it our tafk, from the dictates of our
" religion, the laws of our warfare, and
" the principles and intereft of our policy,
" to regulate your paffions when they over-
" bear, to point out where it is nobler to
" fpare than to revenge, to difcriminate
" degrees of guilt, to fufpend the uplifted
" ftroke, to chaftife and not to deftroy.
" This

"This war to you my friends is new;
" upon all former occasions, in taking
" the field, you held yourselves authorized
" to destroy wherever you came, because
" every where you found an enemy. The
" case is now very different.

" The King has many faithful subjects
" dispersed in the provinces, consequently
" you have many brothers there, and these
" people are more to be pitied, that they
" are persecuted or imprisoned wherever
" they are discovered or suspected, and to
" dissemble, to a generous mind, is a yet
" more grievous punishment.

" Persuaded that your magnanimity of
" character, joined to your principles of
" affection to the King, will give me fuller
" controul over your minds, than the mili-
" tary rank with which I am invested. I en-
" join your most serious attention to the
" rules which I hereby proclaim for your
                                    " invariable

" invariable obfervation during the cam-
" paign."

After anfwering, *Etow! Etow!* in their language fignifying approbation, they appeared to pay very great attention to the interpreter, eager to catch the General's inftructions.

" I pofitively forbid blood-fhed, when
" you are not oppofed in arms.

" Aged men, women, children and pri-
" foners, muft be held facred from the
" knife or hatchet, even in the time of
" actual conflict.

" You fhall receive compenfation for
" the prifoners you take, but you fhall
" be called to account for fcalps.

" In conformity and indulgence of your
" cuftoms, which have affixed an idea of
" honor

" honor to such badges of victory, you
" shall be allowed to take the scalps of the
" dead, when killed by your fire and in
" fair opposition; but on no account, or
" pretence, or subtilty, or prevarication,
" are they to be taken from the wounded,
" or even dying; and still less pardonable,
" if possible, will it be held, to kill men in
" that condition, on purpose, and upon a
" supposition that this protection to the
" wounded would be thereby evaded.

" Base, lurking assassins, incendiaries,
" ravagers and plunderers of the country,
" to whatever army they may belong, shall
" be treated with less reserve; but the lati-
" tude must be given you by order, and I
" must be the judge on the occasion.

" Should the enemy, on their parts, dare
" to countenance acts of barbarity towards
" those who may fall into their hands, it
" shall be yours also to retaliate: but till
" this

" this feverity be thus compelled, bear im-
" moveable in your hearts this folid maxim,
" (it cannot be too deeply impreffed) that
" the great effential reward, the worthy
" fervice of your alliance, the fincerity of
" your zeal to the King, your father and
" never-failing protector, will be examined
" and judged upon the teft only of your
" fteady and uniform adherence to the
" orders and counfels of thofe to whom
" his Majefty has entrufted the direction
" and honor of his arms."

After the General had finifhed his fpeech, they all of them cried out, *Etow! Etow! Etow!* and after remaining fome little time in confultation, an old Chief of the *Iroquois* rofe up, and made the following anfwer:

" I ftand up in the name of all the na-
" tions prefent to affure our father, that
" we have attentively liftened to his dif-
" courfe---

" courfe---we receive you as our father,
" becaufe when you fpeak we hear the voice
" of our great father beyond the great lake.

" We rejoice in the approbation you have
" expreffed of our behaviour.

" We have been tried and tempted by
" the Boftonians; but we have loved our
" father, and our hatchets have been
" fharpened upon our affections.

" In proof of the fincerity of our pro-
" feffions, our whole villages, able to go
" to war, are come forth. The old and
" infirm, our infants and wives, alone re-
" main at home.

" With one common affent, we promife
" a conftant obedience to all you have
" ordered, and all you fhall order, and
" may the father of days give you many,
" and fuccefs."

After the Chief of the *Iroquois* had finifhed, they all as before cried out, *Etow! Etow! Etow!* and the meeting broke up.

One of the General's Aid-de-Camps informed me, that the General was highly pleafed to find the Indians fo tractable, hoping the effential fervice to be expected, would be obtained in employing them. It is through the friendfhip of Captain ****, who took the fpeeches down, that I am enabled to fend them to you.

Orders being given that the army is to embark to-morrow at day-break, to proceed up the lake, and having many things to adjuft, I hope you will pardon my making a hafty conclufion, and remain,

Yours, &c.

An Indian Warrior Entering his Wigwam with a Scalp.

LETTER XXVIII.

Camp at Button-Mole-Bay,
upon Lake Champlain, } June 24, 1777.

MY DEAR FRIEND,

AFTER the meeting of the Indians at river *Bouquet*, the General ordered them some liquor, and they had a war-dance, in which they throw themselves in various postures, every now and then making most hideous yells; as to their appearance, nothing more horrid can you paint to your imagination, being dressed in such an *outré* manner, some with the skins of bulls with the horns upon their heads, others with a great quantity of feathers, and many in a state of total nudity: there was one among them at whofe modefty I could not help fmiling, and who, rather than be divefted of any covering, had tied a blackbird before him. Joined to thefe ftrange dreffes, and added to the grotefque appearance, they paint their faces of various colors, with a view to infpire an additional horror. It is almoft incredible to think what a prodigious degree of conceit and foppery reigns amongft the favages in decorating their perfons, perhaps not inferior to that by which alone fome of our pretty fellows of the prefent age fo confpicuoufly diftinguifh themfelves. The following ftriking inftance of it, feveral other officers, as well as myfelf, were eye-witneffes to, and it afforded us no fmall entertainment:

In our way to their encampment, we obferved a young Indian who was preparing for the war-dance, feated under a *wigwam*, with a fmall looking-glafs placed before him,

him, and surrounded with several papers, filled with different paints. At our stopping to observe him, he was at first a little disconcerted, and appeared displeased, but soon after proceeded to adorn himself. He first smeared his face with a little bear's greafe, then rubbed in some vermillion, then a little black, blue, and green paints, and having viewed himself for some time in the glass, in a rage he wiped it all off, and began again, but with no better success, still appearing dissatisfied. We went on to the council, which lasted near two hours, and on our return found the Indian in the same position, and at the same employment, having nearly consumed all his stock of colors! What a pity it is the ladies in England, adepts in this art, have not such a variety of tints to exercise their genius with!---in my mind, if they must paint, the more ridiculous they appear, the better.

Bear's greafe, indeed, would not be a very delicate perfume, but no matter—— if nature muft be patched up, it little fignifies with what!——I could laugh at the ftreaks on an Indian, but am ftruck with contempt at the airs put on by your flirts, from a penny-worth of carmine, and touched with pity when *fixty* would affume the glow of *fifteen*, through a falfe fhame, or a childifh want of admiration!

An Indian's idea of war confifts in never fighting in an open field, but upon fome very extraordinary occafion, for they confider this method as unworthy an able warrior, and as an affair in which fortune governs, more than prudence or courage.

They are of effential fervice in either defending or invading a country, being extremely fkilful in the art of furprizing, and watching the motions of an enemy.

On a secret expedition they light no fire to warm themselves, nor prepare their victuals, but subsist merely on the miserable pittance of some of their meal mixed with water; they lie close to the ground all day, and only march in the night; while halting to rest and refresh themselves, scouts are sent out on every side to reconnoitre the country, and beat up every place where they suspect an enemy can lie concealed. Two of the principal things that enable them to find out their enemies, is the smoke of their fires, which they smell at a vast distance, and their tracks, in the discovery and distinguishing of which they are possessed of a sagacity equally astonishing, for they will discern by the footsteps, that to us would appear extremely confused, nearly the number of men, and the length of time since they passed; this latter circumstance was confirmed to me by an officer, who has the superintending of their tribes. Being out upon a scout with them

them, they difcerned fome footfteps, when the Indians told him that feven or eight people had paffed that way, and that only two or three days fince: they had not gone far, before they came to a plantation with a houfe upon it, and as is the cuftom with the Indians, ran up to it, and furprized a fcouting party of the Americans, confifting of feven, who had come there the over-night.

In travelling through the woods, they carefully obferve the trees, efpecially the tall pines, which are for the moft part void of foliage, on the branches that are expofed to the north wind, the trunk on that fide having the bark extremely rugged, by which they afcertain the direction to be taken; and for the more eafy difcovery of their way back again, their tomahawks are continually blazing the trees, which is cutting off a fmall piece of the bark, and

as

as they march along they break down the underwood.

Every Indian is a hunter, and their manner of making war is of the same nature, only changing the object, by skulking, surprizing and killing those of their own species, instead of the brute creation.

There is an indisputable necessity of having Indians, where Indians are employed against you, unless we had men enough of our own trained up in that sort of military exercise, as our European discipline is of little avail in the woods against savages.

The reason of my dwelling so much on the subject of Indians, is because I am sensible how repugnant it is to the feelings of an Englishman to employ them, and how much their cruelty and barbarity has been exaggerated.

They

They fight, as those oppofed againft them fight; we muft ufe the fame means as our enemies, to be but on an equal footing with them. I often reflect on that laconic fpeech a great and gallant officer made to his men, in the laft war, previous to their going to battle, " there, my brave lads, " there's the enemy, and, by God, if you " do not kill them, they'll kill you."

There is a very great natural curiofity upon Lake *Champlain*; I am led to imagine that it was originally two lakes. About the center of it the land contracts to fuch a degree, that it appears as if the rock had been feparated by an earthquake; the paffage between what are now two rocks, was but juft wide enough for our large fhips to pafs through, and that only with a fair wind, on account of the current. You'll allow the place to be very juftly named Split-Rock.

This

This bay, where our prefent encampment is, lies on the fouth fide of the lake, and derives its name from the pebbles, of which great abundance are thrown up on the fhores, the exact form of a buttonmould, and where thofe of wood or horn could not be procured, would be no bad fubftitute.

Juft before we entered this bay, there came on a moft violent and unexpected fquall, occafioned by the land winds blowing from the top of the high mountains on the north fide of the lake; it was but of fhort duration, but very terrible while it lafted. You will form fome idea how powerful, and with what violence it blows from thefe mountains, from the following circumftance: A fmall brig belonging to the fleet, with very little fail, was in an inftant laid flat on her fide, and the crew were obliged to cut away the mafts, to make her rife again. The lake was vaftly
agitated,

agitated, you may eafily judge how very dangerous it muft have been to the fmall *batteaux*, which are conftructed with flat bottoms, and quite ungovernable when it blows hard. Though the men who rowed the *batteaux* in which I was were continually relieved, it was with much difficulty they could bring her into this bay, their ftrength being almoft exhaufted. However, the whole brigade got fafe, except two *batteaux* that were fwamped juft as they got clofe in fhore, but as it was not out of a man's depth, no lives were loft.

During this ftorm I dreaded much for the fate of the Indians in their birch canoes, whom I thought muft have inevitably been funk; upon reflection, indeed, they did not feem to be in fuch perfonal danger, as both male and female, above the ftate of infancy, are eternally in the water; to the furprize of every one, however, their canoes rofe to every wave, and floated like a cork;

a cork, which muſt be entirely owing to the lightneſs of their conſtruction; this lightneſs obliged them to remain ſome time upon the lake after we had landed, leſt the waves ſhould daſh their canoes againſt the ſhore and deſtroy them.

I omitted to mention in my laſt, that at the mouth of the river *Bouquet* there is a ſmall iſland, on which were found ſeveral young fawns, where the does had ſwam acroſs to drop them, as if by a natural inſtinct ſenſible that the buck would deſtroy her young. A ſoldier of the company, who had been on this iſland, got one, which he preſented to his Captain; it was beautifully marked, and ſo young, that it could ſcarcely walk; we put it on board the *batteaux*, but during the ſtorm it was waſhed overboard, and every effort to ſave it proved ineffectual, without hazarding the lives of thoſe in the *batteaux*.

Every

Every day, as Addison says, grows

" Big with the fate of Cato and of Rome."

To-morrow we embark from this place to Crown Point, where our operations commence against the enemy. Rest assured I shall embrace every opportunity of sending you the particulars of our proceeding.

Yours, &c.

LETTER XXIX.

Camp at Crown Point, June 30, 1777.

MY DEAR FRIEND,

WE are now within fight of the enemy, and their watch-boats are continually rowing about, but beyond the reach of cannon fhot. Before I proceed farther, let me juft relate in what manner the army paffed the lake, which was by brigades, generally advancing from feventeen to twenty miles a day, and regulated in fuch a manner, that the fecond brigade fhould take the encampment of the firft, and fo on fucceffively, for each brigade to fill

fill the ground the other quitted; the time for departure was always at day-break.

One thing appeared to me very fingular, which I am not philofopher enough to account for; in failing up the lake, on all the iflands and points of land, the water feemed to feparate the trees from the land, and to pafs in a manner through them, having the appearance of fmall brufh wood, at a very little heighth from the water; nor do the trees appear to come in contact with the land, till you approach within two or three miles of the object, when they fhow themfelves to be diftinctly joined.

I cannot forbear picturing to your imagination one of the moft pleafing fpectacles I ever beheld. When we were in the wideft part of the lake, whofe beauty and extent I have already defcribed, it was remarkably fine and clear, not a breeze ftirring,

ftirring, when the whole army appeared at one view in fuch perfect regularity, as to form the moft compleat and fplendid regatta you can poffibly conceive. A fight fo novel and pleafing, could not fail of fixing the admiration and attention of every one prefent.

In the front, the Indians went with their birch canoes, containing twenty or thirty in each, then the advanced corps in a regular line, with the gun-boats, then followed the Royal George and Inflexible, towing large booms, which are to be thrown acrofs two points of land, with the other brigs and floops following; after them the firft brigade in a regular line, then the Generals Burgoyne, Phillips, and Reidefel in their pinnaces; next to them were the fecond brigade, followed by the German brigades, and the rear was brought up with the futlers and followers of the army. Upon the appearance of fo
for-

formidable a fleet, you may imagine they were not a little difmayed at Ticonderoga, for they were apprized of our advance, as we every day could fee their watch-boats. We had, it is certain, a very ftrong naval force, but yet it might have been greatly in the power of the Americans to have prevented our paffing the lake fo rapidly as we have done, efpecially as there are certain parts of it where a few armed veffels might have ftopped us for fome time: but it is an invariable maxim with the Americans, of which there are numberlefs inftances in the laft campaign, never to face an enemy but with very fuperior advantages, and the moft evident figns and profpects of fuccefs.

The army is now affembling in order to commence the fiege, as foon as the artillery ftores arrive from Canada, which are daily expected. People in England, whofe rapidity of ideas keep pace with their good
wifhes,

wishes, little imagine that the distance from this place to Canada is ninety miles, therefore the time it takes to bring forward stores is necessarily considerable. To the great praise of General Carleton, however, very little delay has yet occurred, for he forwards the stores very expeditiously, and however ill-treated many people suppose he is, or however he may conceive himself so, in not having the command of this army, after being the commander in the last campaign, he lets no pique or ill-will divert him from doing all the real service in his power to his King and country.

In a former letter I mentioned, that we were to intrench at this place: but however measures may be concerted with the utmost judgment and precaution for succeeding, yet when an army has advanced to the place they are to invest, the General is often convinced, that neither the description of others, nor the delineation of maps and charts have been so perfect in every particular, as not to make some change in the intended dispositions necessary, which is exactly our present situation, as orders are given out for us to embark to-morrow. What will be the future operations of the army, after the reduction of Ticonderoga, it is impossible to say, but some vigorous measures, no doubt, are to be pursued, as an extract from the General's orders will point out to you. It is generally believed, however, that the army is to force its way into Albany. The extract is as follows:

" This army embarks to-morrow to ap-
" proach the enemy. The services re-
" quired of this particular expedition, are
" critical and conspicuous. During our
" progress occasions may occur, in which
" nor difficulty, nor labor, nor life are to
" be regarded. This army must not re-
" treat." From the last sentence, it is a general and fixed opinion throughout the
whole

whole army, that vigorous exertions are to be made againſt any oppoſition, however ſuperior, we may encounter. For ſuch an expedition the army are in the beſt condition that can be expected or wiſhed, the troops in the higheſt ſpirits, admirably diſciplined, and remarkably healthy.

I omitted to mention, that ſhortly after the conſultation with the Indians at the river *Bouquet*, the General iſſued out a manifeſto, which was circulated in the frontiers and province of Connecticut, calculated to ſpread terror among the moſt rebellious, to enforce upon their minds an impreſſion of fear, of the cruel operations of ſavages, whom he now could reſtrain, and their eagerneſs to be let looſe; at the ſame time, in the moſt expreſſive language, informing them, that powerful forces were co-operating, both by ſea and land, to cruſh this unnatural rebellion; inveighing ſtrongly on the conduct of the preſent

Gover-

Governors and Governments here as being the cauſe of its continuance, and exhibiting, in the moſt lively manner, their injuſtice, cruelty, perſecution and tyranny; encouraging thoſe whoſe diſpoſition and abilities would aſſiſt in redeeming their country from ſlavery, and re-eſtabliſhing its former government; offering protection and ſecurity to thoſe who continued peaceable in their habitations, and denouncing all the calamities and outrages of war to ſuch as ſhould perſevere in hoſtilities. How far it may operate in this part of the continent, I have my fears, as the New-England Provinces are the moſt violent in their principles of rebellion.

During our ſtay at this place, which has been only three days, the rear of the army is come up, and the magazines and hoſpitals are eſtabliſhed, therefore the operations againſt Ticonderoga will immediately commence.

I am

I am truly sensible how averse you were to my entering the army, but when once immerged, it would be folly in the extreme to say, that I wished to retract. Although I am not an enthusiast in religion, still you know I ever held in the greatest veneration the supreme Disposer of Events, and am not insensible of his protecting hand, a soldier has many hair-breadth escapes; but should it be the fate of war, and the will of Providence that I should fall, I shall die with the pleasing reflection of having served my King and country. If I survive, you may rest assured of my embracing every opportunity to inform you of my destiny, and how truly I am,

Yours, &c.

LETTER XXX.

Camp before Ticonderoga, July 5, 1777.

MY DEAR FRIEND,

WE are now arrived before a place that is not more talked of this war than the laſt, on account of the memorable ſiege that then happened, in which that gallant officer was ſlain, who, could his immortal ſpirit riſe from its cold manſion, would no doubt be highly pleaſed to ſee his offspring, one placed at the head of naval line, and the other of the army, advancing the pleaſing taſk of reſtoring peace to a deluded people, led on by a ſet of of factious men, to a moſt unnatural rebellion.

By the ſcouting parties juſt returned we learn, that there is a brigade which occupies the old French lines on a height, to the north of the fort of Ticonderoga; the lines are in good repair, with ſeveral intrenchments behind them, ſupported by a block-houſe; they have another poſt at the ſaw-mills, the foot of the carrying-place to Lake George, and a block-houſe upon an eminence above the mills, together with a block-houſe and hoſpital at the entrance of the lake.

Upon the right of the lines, between them and the old fort, are two new block-houſes, and a conſiderable battery cloſe to the water's edge. But it ſeems the Americans have employed their utmoſt induſtry where they are in the greateſt force, upon Mount Independence, which is extremely lofty

lofty and circular. On the fummit of the mount they have a ftar fort made of pickets, well fupplied with artillery, and a large fquare of barracks within it; that fide of the hill which projects into the lake is well intrenched, and has a ftrong abattis clofe to the water, which is lined with heavy artillery pointing down the lake, flanking the water battery, and fuftained by another about half way up the hill. Fortified as the enemy are, nothing but a regular fiege can difpoffefs them.

There has been a fkirmifh with the Indians and a fmall party of the enemy, who were reconnoitering, in which they were driven back into their lines; the Indians were fo rafh as to purfue them within reach of their cannon, when feveral were killed and wounded. Upon the firing of their artillery, the brigade were ordered under arms, and fhortly after the Indians brought the killed and wounded upon litters,

ters, covered with leaves. It was thought this would have been a check upon them, as the firſt that fell was of their party, but it ſeems rather to ſtimulate their valor.

As our friend M--- was looking through a braſs reflecting teleſcope at the enemy's works, he cried out ſhot, and we had ſcarcely dropt down, before we were covered with duſt. He ſaw them run out the cannon of the embraſure, and what I imagine contributed to their pointing them, was the reflection of the ſun upon the teleſcope. After they had diſcovered our ſituation, they fired ſeveral ſhot, but without doing any miſchief.

A very ſingular circumſtance has occured at this encampment. This morning, a little after day-break, the centinel of the picquet guard ſaw a man in the woods, reading a book, whom the centinel challenged, but being ſo very intent on his
                                ſtudies,

studies, he made no reply, when the soldier ran up to, and seized him; upon waking from his reverie, he told the centinel he was Chaplain to the 47th regiment, but it being a suspicious circumstance, he was detained till the soldier was relieved, who took him to the Captain of the picquet, from whence he was immediately sent to General Frafer's quarters. General Frafer suppofing it was a finefle, for the 47th regiment was stationed two or three miles in the rear, and the General thinking himself perfectly acquainted with every clergyman in the army, began to make feveral enquiries concerning the Americans, at which he was more perplexed, and still perfifted in his firft ftory. What greatly contributed to thefe miftakes, the man's appearance was not altogether in his favor, being in difhabille. General Frafer not being able to make any thing of him, fent him with an officer to General Burgoyne, who had no knowledge of him.

To

To clear up the matter, the Colonel of the 47th regiment was sent for, who informed the General that he was the gentleman who had delivered a letter from General Carleton, and had only joined the regiment from Canada the preceding evening. The studious gentleman little foresaw to what dangers he had exposed himself by his morning ramble, till he was stopped by the centinel. You will naturally think he had enough to cure him from these perambulations in the woods.

About three days since a great smoke was observed towards Lake George, and the scouts brought in a report, that the enemy had set fire to the farthest blockhouse, had abandoned the saw-mills, and that a considerable body was advancing from the lines towards a bridge, upon a road which led from the saw-mills to the right of our encampment. A detachment from our corps, supported by the second brigade

brigade, and fome light artillery, under the command of General Phillips, were then ordered to proceed to Mount Hope, to reconnoitre the enemy's pofition, and to take advantage of any poſt they might either abandon or be driven from.

The Indians under the command of Captain Frazer, fupported by his company of markfmen, (which were volunteer companies from each regiment of the Britiſh) were directed to make a circuit on the left of our encampment, to cut off the retreat of the enemy to their lines : this defign, however, was fruſtrated by the impetuofity of the Indians, who attacked too foon, which enabled the enemy to retire with little lofs. General Phillips took Mount Hope, which cut off the enemy from any communication with Lake George; after which we quitted our former encampment, and occupied this poſt, which is now in great force, there being the whole of General

neral Frafer's corps, **the firft** Britifh brigade, and two brigades of **artillery**. The enemy have cannonaded the **camp**, but without effect, and continued the fame the next day, while the army were employed in getting up the artillery tents, baggage, and provifions, during which time we never fired a fingle cannon.

This day Luitenant Twifs, the commanding engineer, was ordered to reconnoitre Sugar-Hill, on the fouth fide of **the communication from Lake George into Lake Champlain**, part of which the light-infantry had taken poffeffion of laft night; he reported this hill to have the entire command of the works and buildings, both at Ticonderoga and Mount Independence, of about 1400 yards from the former, and 1500 from the latter; that the ground might be levelled fo as to receive cannon, and that the road to convey them, though extremely difficult, might be

accom-

accomplished in twenty-four hours. This hill also commanded the bridge of communication, and from it they could see the exact situation of their vessels; and what was another very great advantage, from **the possession** of this post, the enemy, during the day, could not make any material movement or preparation, without being discovered, and even their numbers counted. Upon this report of Lieutenant **Twiss, it was determined a battery** should be raised on this post, for light twenty-four pounders, medium twelves, and eight inch howitzers, which very arduous undertaking is now carrying on so rapidly, that there is little doubt but it will be compleated and ready to open upon the enemy to-morrow morning. Great praise is due to the zeal and activity of General Phillips, who has the direction of this operation: he has as expeditiously conveyed cannon to the summit of this hill, as he brought it up in that memorable

battle

battle at Minden, where, it is said, such was his anxiousness in expediting the artillery, that he split no less than fifteen canes in beating the horses; at which battle he so gallantly distinguished himself, by the management of his artillery, as totally to rout the French.

I am happy to embrace the opportunity of sending this by a sutler, who is returning down the lake to St. John's. Be assured you shall know every event of this important siege, by the first conveyance that presents itself. Adieu.

Yours, &c.

LETTER XXXI.

Camp at Skenesborough, July 12, 1777.

MY DEAR FRIEND,

NO doubt, after so much as I have repeatedly mentioned to you in my former letters relative to Ticonderoga, and the vigorous defence it was universally supposed the enemy would make, you will be greatly surprized to receive a letter from me, at so great a distance beyond that important post; fully to explain to you the manner of the Americans abandoning it, and our progress to this place, I must proceed a little methodically in my description.

After

After we had gained poffeffion of Sugar-Hill, on the 5th inftant, that very evening we obferved the enemy making great fires; it was then generally thought they were meditating an attack, or that they were retreating, which latter circumftance really was the cafe, for about day-break intelligence was brought to General Frafer, that the enemy were retiring, when the picquets were ordered to advance, which the brigades, as foon as they were accoutred, were to follow.

They were foon ready, and marched down to the works; when we came to the bridge of communication, we were obliged to halt till it was fufficiently repaired for the troops to pafs, as the enemy, in their abandoning the works, had deftroyed it, and had left four men, who were, upon the approach of our army, to have fired off the cannon of a large battery that defended it,

and

and retire as quick as poffible. No doubt this was their intention, as they left their lighted matches clofe to the cannon.

Had thefe men obeyed their inftructions, they would, fituated as our brigade was, have done great mifchief; but, allured by the fweets of plunder and liquor, inftead of obeying their orders, we found them **dead drunk by a cafk of Madeira**. This battery, however, had, through the folly of an Indian, nearly been productive of fatal confequences to the 9th regiment, for juft at the time it was paffing the bridge, as he was very curious in examining every thing that came in his way, he took up a match that lay on the ground, with fome fire ftill remaining in it, when a fpark dropping upon the priming of a cannon, it went off, loaded with all manner of combuftibles, but it fortunately happened the gun was fo elevated, no mifchief enfued.

Shortly

In a ſhort time after the bridge was rendered paſſable, our brigade croſſed, and we advanced up to the picqueted fort, where the Britiſh colours were inſtantly hoiſted. The Americans certainly had planned ſome ſcheme, which proved abortive, and which was left perhaps to the commiſſion of thoſe men who remained behind, for the ground was ſtrewed all over with gunpowder, and there were likewiſe ſeveral caſks of it with the tops ſtruck out.

After we had remained ſome little time in the fort, orders came for the advanced corps to march in purſuit of the enemy, who, we were informed, had gone to Huberton, in order to harraſs their rear. We marched till one o'clock, in a very hot and ſultry day, over a continued ſucceſſion of ſteep and woody hills; the diſtance I cannot aſcertain, but we were marching very expeditiously from four in the morning to that time.

On our march we picked up several stragglers, from whom General Frafer learnt that the rear-guard of the enemy was compofed of chofen men, commanded by a Colonel Francis, who was reckoned one of their beft officers.

During the time the advanced corps halted to refrefh, General Reidefel came up, and after confulting with General Frafer, and making arrangements for continuing the purfuit, we marched forward again three miles nearer the enemy, to an advantageous fituation, where we lay that night on our arms.

At three in the morning our march was renewed, and about five we came up with the enemy, who were bufily employed in cooking their provifions.

Major

Major Grant, of the 24th regiment, who had the advanced guard, attacked their picquets, which were foon driven in to the main body. From this attack we lament the death of this very gallant and brave officer, who in all probability fell a victim to the great difadvantages we experience peculiar to this unfortunate conteft, thofe of the rifle-men. Upon his coming up with the enemy, he got upon the ftump of a tree to reconnoitre, and had hardly given the men orders to fire, when he was ftruck by a rifle ball, fell off the tree, and never uttered another fyllable.

The light infantry then formed, as well as the 24th regiment, the former of which fuffered very much from the enemy's fire, particularly the companies of the 29th and 34th regiments. The grenadiers were ordered to form to prevent the enemy's getting to the road that leads to Caftle-Town, which they were endeavouring to do, and were

were repulsed, upon which they attempted their retreat by a very steep mountain to Pittsford. The grenadiers scrambled up an ascent which appeared almost inaccessible, and gained the summit of the mountain before them; this threw them into great confusion, and that you may form some idea how steep the ascent must have been, the men were obliged to sling their firelocks and climb up the side, sometimes resting their feet upon the branch of a tree, and sometimes on a piece of the rock; had any been so unfortunate as to have missed his hold, he must inevitably been dashed to pieces.

Although the grenadiers had gain'd the summit of this mountain, and the Americans had lost great numbers of their men, with their brave commander Col. Francis, still they were far superior in numbers to the British, and the contest remained doubtful till the arrival of the Germans, when

when the Americans fled on all sides, whose numbers amounted to 2000; they were opposed only by 850 British, as it was near two hours before the Germans made their appearance.

General Reidesel had come to the field of action a considerable time before his troops, and in the course of the action passing by him, I could not help feeling for his situation, for the honor of a brave officer, who was pouring forth every imprecation against his troops, for their not arriving at the place of action time enough to earn the glories of the day.

Upon their arrival, we were apprehensive, by the noise we heard, that a reinforcement had been sent back from the main body of the American army for the support of their rear-guard, for they began singing psalms on their advance, and at the same time kept up an incessant firing, which

which totally decided the fate of the day; but even after the action was over, there were lurking parties hovering about the woods.

During the battle the Americans were guilty of such a breach of all military rules, as could not fail to exasperate our soldiers. The action was chiefly in woods, interspersed with a few open fields. Two companies of grenadiers, who were stationed in the skirts of the wood, close to one of these fields, to watch that the enemy did not out-flank the 24th regiment, observed a number of the Americans, to the amount of near sixty, coming across the field, with their arms clubbed, which is always considered to be a surrender as prisoners of war. The grenadiers were restrained from firing, commanded to stand with their arms, and shew no intention of hostility: when the Americans had got within ten yards, they in an instant turned round
their

their mufquets, fired upon the grenadiers, and run as faft as they could into the woods; their fire killed and wounded a great number of men, and thofe who efcaped immediately purfued them, and gave no quarter.

This war is very different to the laft in Germany; in this the life of an individual is fought with as much avidity as the obtaining a victory over an army of thoufands, of which the following is a melancholy inftance.

After the action was over, and all firing had ceafed for near two hours, upon the fummit of the mountain I have already defcribed, which had no ground any where that could command it, a number of officers were collected to read the papers taken out of the pocket book of Colonel Francis, when Captain Shrimpton, of the 62d regiment, who had the papers in his hand,
jumped

jumped up and fell, exclaiming, " he was " feverely wounded;" we all heard the ball whiz by us, and turning to the place from whence the report came, faw the fmoke: as there was every reafon to imagine the piece was fired from fome tree, a party of men were inftantly detached, but could find no perfon, the fellow, no doubt, as foon as he had fired, had flipt down and made his efcape.

About five o'clock in the afternoon, the grenadiers were ordered from the fummit of the mountain to join the light infantry and 24th regiment, on an advantageous fituation; in our cool moments, in defcending, every one was aftonifhed how he had ever gained the fummit.— For my own part, it appeared as if I fhould never reach the bottom; but my defcent was greatly retarded by conducting Major Ackland, who was wounded in the thigh.

In

In this action I found all manual exercife is but an ornament, and the only object of importance it can boaft of was that of loading, firing, and charging with bayonets: as to the former, the foldiers fhould be inftructed in the beft and moft expeditious method. Here I cannot help obferving to you, whether it proceeded from an idea of felf prefervation, or natural inftinct, but the foldiers greatly improved the mode they were taught in, as to expedition, for as foon as they had primed their pieces, and put the cartridge into the barrel, inftead of ramming it down with their rods, they ftruck the butt end of their piece upon the ground, and bringing it to the *prefent*, fired it off. The confufion of a man's ideas during the time of action, brave as he may be, is undoubtedly great; feveral of the men, upon examining their mufkets, after all was over, found five or fix cartridges, which

which they were pofitive to the having difcharged.

Deferring the remainder of the particulars of this action, with our march to this place, I remain

Yours, &c.

LETTER XXXII.

Camp at Skenesborough, July 14, 1777.

MY DEAR FRIEND,

THE confusion of the enemy on their retreat was very great, as they were neither sensible where they fled, nor by whom they were conducted, after Colonel Francis was killed, when they took to the mountains.

Exclusive of 200 men that were killed, and near 600 wounded, many of whom died in endeavouring to get off, the loss on our side has been very inconsiderable. After the action was over, a Colonel with
the

the remains of his regiment, to the amount of 230, came and surrendered himself prisoner.

The advantages of the ground was wholly on the side of the Americans, added to which the woods were so thick, that little or no order could be observed in advancing upon the enemy, it being totally impossible to form a regular line; personal courage and intrepidity was therefore to supply the place of military skill and discipline. The native bravery of our countrymen could not be more resolutely displayed than in this action, nor more effectually exerted. It was a trial of the activity, strength and valor of every man that fought. At the commencement of the action the enemy were every where thrown into the greatest confusion, but being rallied by that brave officer, Colonel Francis, whose death, though an enemy, will ever be regretted by those who can feel for the
loss

loss of a gallant and brave man; the fight was renewed with the greatest degree of fierceness and obstinacy. Both parties engaged in separate detachments unconnected with each other, and the numbers of the enemy empowered them to front flank and rear. Some of these detachments, notwithstanding an inferiority, most resolutely defended themselves, and the fate of the day was undecided till the arrival of the Germans, who, though late, came in for a share of the glory, in difperfing the enemy in all quarters.

Having given you the particulars of this engagement, permit me, as it is the firft I ever was in, to make my remarks in the time of conflict.

During the action, every apprehenfion and idea of danger forfakes the mind, which becomes more animated and determined the nearer the time of attack approaches.

Every

Every soldier feels inspired with an impatient ardor, as if he conceived the fate of the battle would be decided by the level of his musquet, or the point of his bayonet: but the conflict once over, the mind returns to its proper sense of feeling, and deeply must its sensibility be wounded, when the eye glances over the field of slaughter, where so many brave fellows, who a few hours before were in high spirits and full of the vigor of life, are laid low in the dust; and the ear continually pierced with the deep sighs and groans of the wounded and dying. Even the joy rising in the bosom at the sight of surviving friends and brother officers, is saddened by the recollection of those who fell. Such, my dear friend, are the sensations of the mind, before and after a battle.

That soldiers have many hair-breadth escapes, I am sure was never more fully

verified

verified, than in regard to Lord Balcarres, who commands the light infantry; he had near thirty balls fhot through his jacket and trowfers, and yet only received a fmall graze on the hip. Others were equally, as unfortunate, for upon the very firft attack of the light infantry, Lieutenant Haggit received a ball in each of his eyes, and Lieutenant Douglas, of the 29th regiment, as he was carried off the field wounded, received a ball directly through his heart. Thefe extraordinary events may in fome meafure be accounted for, as the leaft refiftance of a mufquet ball will give it a direction almoft incredible: when the Surgeon came to examine the wound of a poor American, it appeared that the ball had entered on his left fide, and having traverfed between the fkin and the back bone, came out on the oppofite fide.

When General Frafer had pofted the corps in an advantageous ftate of defence, and made fome log works, as he expected we fhould be attacked, his next thoughts were, how to refrefh the men after the fatigues of the day, provifions being unable to be forwarded, on account of the country's being very hilly; a detachment was fent to fhoot fome bullocks that were running in the woods, thefe were diftributed in ratios to the men, which they eat, dreffed upon wood afhes, without either bread or falt.

Juft at this time chance fupplied the officers with a very acceptable, though fingular fubftitute for bread to their beef: an officer who was at Ticonderoga, by way of a joke, fent his brother a great quantity of gingerbread that was taken at that place, which he now diftributed among the officers, and as General Frafer fhared the
fame

fame as the men, he sent part of it to him as a present.

We laid upon our arms all night, and the next morning sent back the prisoners to Ticonderoga, amounting to near 250. A very small detachment could be spared to guard them, as General Fraser expected the enemy would have reinforcements from the main body of their army, and oppose his crossing a wide creek, after we had passed Castletown. He told the Colonel of the Americans, who had surrendered himself, to inform the rest of the prisoners, that if they attempted to escape, no quarter would be shewn them, and that those who might elude the guard, the Indians would be sent in pursuit of, and scalp them.

Leaving the sick and wounded under the care of a subaltern's guard, to protect them from the Indians, or scouting parties of the enemy, the brigade marched to Castle-

Caſtletown, where the men were recruited with ſome freſh proviſions and a gill of rum; after this they proceeded on their march to the creek, to croſs over which the pioneers were obliged to fell ſome trees; only one man could paſs over at a time, ſo that it was near dark before the whole of the brigade had croſſed, when we had ſeven miles to march to this place.

Major Shrimpton, who I told you was wounded upon the hill, rather than remain with the wounded at Huberton, preferred marching with the brigade, and on croſſing this creek, having only one hand to aſſiſt himſelf with, was on the point of ſlipping in, had not an officer who was behind him caught hold of his cloaths, juſt as he was falling. His wound was through his ſhoulder, and as he could walk, he ſaid he would not remain to fall into the enemy's hands, as it was univerſally thought the ſick and wounded muſt. Very fortunately,

nately, however, for them, they met with no moleftation, and three days after were conveyed in litters to Ticonderoga, as the road was impaffable for any fort of carriage.

After we had croffed the creek, General Frafer was perfectly eafy in his mind concerning an attack, which he had been apprehenfive of the whole day, and gave orders to make the beft of our way to this encampment, which was through a road where every ftep we took was nearly up to the knees. After a march of near thirty miles, in an exceffive woody and bad country, every moment in expectation of being attacked, till we had croffed the creek, you muft naturally fuppofe we underwent a moft fevere fatigue, both of mind and body.

For my own part, I readily own to you, that the exertions of the day had fo far

Z 4   wearied

wearied me, that drinking heartily of rum and water, I laid down in my bear-fkin and blanket, and did not awake till twelve the next day. But that I may not fatigue you as much as I then felt myfelf, or make you fall afleep, I fhall conclude with fubfcribing myfelf,

Yours, &c.

LETTER XXXIII.

Camp at Skenesborough, July 14, 1777.

MY DEAR FRIEND,

WE are still encamped at this place, waiting the arrival of provisions, *batteaux*, and many other incumbrances, armies in general are but very seldom troubled with, and is a hindrance which that to the southward has not to encounter, for whatever want of water carriage they meet with, the navy can always act in co-operation with them. I mention this, that you may not be surprized at our not making such rapid marches, and over-

over-running the country, as they in all probability will.

The army are all affembled at this place, and in a few days the advanced corps march to Fort Edward. You would like to learn the movements of the other part of the army, after we got poffeffion of Ticonderoga; I was not with them, but you fhall know what I have been able to collect.

After a paffage had been made, with great difficulty, but with much expedition, for the gun-boats and veffels to pafs the bridge of communication, between Ticonderoga and Fort Independence, (which had coft the Americans much labor and expence in conftructing) the main body of the army purfued the enemy by South Bay, within three miles of this place, where they were pofted in a ftockaded fort, with their armed gallies. The firft

brigade

brigade was difembarked with an intention of cutting off the enemy's retreat, but their hafty flight rendered that manœuvre ufelefs. The gun-boats and frigates purfued the armed veffels, and when the enemy arrived at the falls of this place, they made a defence for fome time, after which they blew up three of their veffels, and the other two ftruck.

On the enemy's retreat they fet fire to the fort, dwelling-houfe, faw-mill, ironworks, and all the building on this plantation, deftroyed the *batteaux* and retired to Fort Edward.

An officer who came up at the time of the conflagration, affured me he never faw fo tremendous a fight; for exclufive of the fhipping, building, &c. the trees all up the fide of the hanging rock, had caught fire, as well as at the top of a very lofty hill.

hill. The element appeared to threaten univerfal deftruction.

The 9th regiment was fent to take poft at Fort Ann, to obferve the motion of the enemy, as well as to diflodge them: but intelligence having been received that they had been greatly reinforced, Colonel Hill fent word to General Burgoyne, that he fhould not retire with his regiment but maintain his ground; the other two regiments of the brigade, with two pieces of artillery, were ordered to fupport them, with General Phillips, who took the command; but a violent ftorm of rain, which lafted the whole day, prevented their getting to their relief fo foon as was intended, which gave the 9th regiment an opportunity of diftinguifhing themfelves, in a moft gallant and fignal manner, by repulfing an attack of fix times their number, and the enemy not being able to force

them

them in front, endeavored to turn their flank, which from their great fuperiority was much to be feared; when Colonel Hill thought it neceffary to change his pofition in the very height of the action, which was executed with great fteadinefs and bravery. In this manner the fight was carried on for a confiderable length of time, the Britifh troops maintaining their ground, and the enemy gradually retiring, were at laft totally repulfed, and fled to Fort Edward, fetting fire to Fort Ann, but left a faw-mill and block-houfe ftanding, which was immediately taken poffeffion of by a party of the 9th regiment.

After we had abandoned this block-houfe and faw mills, and proceeded to Fort Edward, the enemy returned and fet fire to it; and as you defire me to fend you a few drawings of fuch things as I might think beft

beft worth taking a fketch of, I have fent a reprefentation of the block-houfe and faw mill, as being a very romantic view.

The 9th regiment have acquired great honor in this action; though it lafted fo long, and was fought under fuch difadvantages, they have fuftained very little lofs. Captain Montgomery (brother-in-law to Lord Townfhend) a very gallant officer, was wounded early in the action, and taken prifoner, with the Surgeon, as he was drefling his wound, which happened as the regiment was changing its pofition.

During this action, that pleafant Hibernian acquaintance of ours, M——, of the fame regiment, was flightly wounded, and conveyed into the houfe with the reft of the wounded, which had been attacked, as part of the regiment had thrown themfelves into it, for better defence during the action. Our friend M——, in endeavoring

Fort Anne Creek the property of Gen'l Skeene.

...na was set fire to by the Americans.
...ane Leadenhall Street London

ing to comfort his fellow-fufferers, in a blunt manner, exclaimed, "By heavens, "my good lads, you need not think fo "much of being wounded, for by Jafus "God there's a bullet in the beam."

As to the other part of the army, fome remained behind at Ticonderoga, fome employed in bringing up the *batteaux*, &c. but the whole are now affembled, and collected at this place.

From the various accounts we have been able to collect of the Americans, relative to their abandoning Ticonderoga, it feemed that upon our gaining poffeffion of Sugar-Hill, a poft which they were certainly very negligent and imprudent in not fecuring, they were greatly difmayed, and feeing the preparations we were making to open a battery, which I before obferved had the command of all their works, they called a council of their principal officers,
when

when it was pointed out to them by General Sinclair, who commanded the garrison, that their force was very deficient in numbers to man their works, and that it was impoſſible to make any effectual defence, obſerving to them that places, however ſtrong, without a ſufficient number of troops, muſt ſurrender, and that in all probability the place would be ſurrounded in leſs than four and twenty hours. In this ſituation of affairs, the General ſaw the ruin of his army, and it was his opinion that the fort ought to be abandoned to ſave the troops; that the baggage and artillery ſtores were to be ſent to Skeneſborough by water, and the troops were to march by land, by the way of Huberton, to that place. Theſe propoſals being fully approved of by the council, was the reaſon of their evacuating it that night, and hazarding the undertaking.

General

General Burgoyne forefeeing the great difficulties of conveying even provifions, fetting apart baggage, has iffued out the following orders:

"It is obferved, that the injunction
"given before the army took the field, re-
"lative to the baggage of officers, has not
"been complied with, and that the regi-
"ments in general are incumbered with
"much more baggage than they can pof-
"fibly be fupplied with means of convey-
"ing, when they quit the lake and rivers:
"warning is therefore given again to the
"officers, to convey by the *batteaux* which
"will foon return to Ticonderoga, the
"baggage that is not indifpenfibly necef-
"fary to them, or upon the firft fudden
"movement, it muft inevitably be left on
"the ground. Such gentlemen as ferved
"in America laft war may remember, that
"the officers took up with foldiers tents,
"and

" and often confined their baggage to a
" knapfack, for months together."

Fortunately for me, my horfe has come fafe round the lakes, which will enable me to keep the little baggage I brought with me.

The Indians, animated with our fuccefs, have acquired more confidence and eourage, as great numbers have joined the army, and are daily continuing fo to do.

Unexpected orders being juft given out, that Captain Gardner departs to-morrow for England, and having feveral more letters to write, I am obliged to leave you. Adieu.

Yours, &c.

LETTER XXXIV.

Camp at Skenesborough, July 17, 1777.

MY DEAR FRIEND,

YOU will no doubt be surprized, that in my account of the proceedings of the army, every circumstance of which seems to add glory and conquest to the British arms, that I never made mention of the savages, in our pursuit of the enemy from Ticonderoga; they could not, in any respect whatever, be drawn away from the plunder of that place, and I am afraid this is not the only instance in which the General has found their assistance little more than a name.

Thofe who have the management and conduct of them are, from interefted motives, obliged to indulge them in all their caprices and humors, and, like fpoiled children, are more unreafonable and importunate upon every new indulgence granted them: but there is no remedy; were they left to themfelves, they would be guilty of enormities too horrid to think of, for guilty and innocent, women and infants, would be their common prey.

This is too much the cafe of the lower Canadian Indians, which are the only ones who have joined our army; but we underftand, within two days march, the *Outawas*, and fome remoter nations, are on the road to join us, more brave, and more tractable, who profefs war, and not pillage. They are under the direction of a *Monfieur St. Luc*, and one *Langdale*, both of whom were great partizans of the French laft war; the latter was the perfon who planned and executed,

executed, with the nations he is now efcorting, the defeat of General Braddock.

If thefe Indians correfpond with the character given of them, fome good may be derived from their affiftance; little is to be expected from thofe with the army at prefent, but plundering.

As I hinted to you in a former letter, the General's manifefto has not had the defired effect, as intelligence is brought in that the committees are ufing their utmoft endeavors to counteract it, by watching and imprifoning all perfons they fufpect, compelling the people to take arms, to drive their cattle and burn their corn, under the penalty of immediate death; and, forry am I to add, that numbers of well-difpofed perfons to the fuccefs of our arms, have already undergone that fate! Hiftory, I think, cannot furnifh an inftance, where a war was ever carried on with fo much rancor, not only with thofe who feem inclined to oppofe them, but equally to thofe who would remain neuter.

Numbers have joined the army fince we have penetrated into this place, profeffing themfelves loyalifts, wifhing to ferve, fome to the end of the war, fome only the campaign, a third part of the number have arms, and till arms arrive for the remainder, they are employed in clearing the roads and repairing the bridges, in which the Americans are very expert.

We are obliged to wait fome time in our prefent pofition, till the roads are cleared of the trees which the Americans felled after their retreat. You would think it almoft impoffible, but every ten or twelve yards great trees are laid acrofs the road, exclufive of fmaller ones, efpecially when it is confidered what a hafty retreat they made of it. Repairing the bridges is a

work

work of some labor, added to which, a stock of provisions must be brought up previous to our marching to Fort Edward. We lie under many disadvantages in prosecuting this war, from the impediments I have stated, and we cannot follow this great military maxim, " in good success push the " advantage as far as you can."

While this part of the army is thus employed, the remainder are conveying the gun-boats, *batteaux* and provision vessels into Lake George, to scour that lake, and secure the future route of our magazines; when that force is ready to move down the lake, the army will proceed to possess Fort Edward, by which means the enemy, if they do not abandon Fort George, must inevitably be caught, as they will be enclosed by the two armies,. During these movements General Reidesel is to make a diversion into Connecticut, and reconnoitre the country, and by that feint to draw the attention of the Americans to almoſt every quarter.

Our ſucceſſes, no doubt, muſt have operated ſtrongly on the minds of the enemy, and they will be equally as anxious to adopt meaſures for ſtopping the progreſs of our army, as to prevent the imminent danger the northern colonies are expoſed to.

On Sunday laſt a thankſgiving ſermon was preached, for the ſucceſs of our arms, after which there was a *feu de joie* fired by the whole army, with artillery and ſmall arms; the ſermon was preached by the clergyman whom I have made mention of, and an exceeding good one it was, for a pariſh church, but not in the leaſt applicable to the occaſion.

By the beſt intelligence that can be gained, we are informed, that General Schuyler is at Fort Edward, collecting the militia

from

from the adjacent countries, which, with the remains of their broken army, is to form a sufficient body for making a stand at this place. Their shattered army have suffered incredible hardships from the want of provisions, and the necessaries to cover them, from the incessant rains that have fell of late, as they were compelled to make a week's circuit through the woods, before they could reach Fort Edward, in order to avoid the various strong detachments that we had in different parts, on the Connecticut side.

I omitted to mention to you, that your old friend Captain H——, was wounded at the battle of Huberton, early in the action, when the grenadiers formed to support the light infantry. I could not pass by him as he lay under a tree, where he had scrambled upon his hands and knees, to protect him from the scattering shot, without going up to see what assistance could be afforded him,

and

and learn if he was feverely wounded. You who know his ready turn for wit, will not be furprized to hear, though in extreme agony, that with an arch look, and clapping his hand behind him, he told me, if I wanted to be fatisfied, I muft afk that, as the ball had entered at his hip, and paffed through a certain part adjoining : he is now at Ticonderoga, and, from the laft account, is recovering faft.

We march to-morrow, and on our arrival at Fort Edward you may depend upon hearing from,

Yours, &c.

LETTER XXXV.

Camp at Fort Edward, August 6, 1777.

MY DEAR FRIEND,

WE are arrived at this place, in which it was thought the enemy would have made a stand, but upon intelligence of our advancing, they precipitately abandoned it, as they did the garrison of Ticonderoga. Very fortunately for the garrison of Fort George, they had passed this place about an hour before our arrival; had they been that much later, they must have been inevitably cut off.

The

The country between our late encampment at Skenefborough and this place, was a continuation of woods and creeks, interfperfed with deep moraffes; and to add to thefe natural impediments, the enemy had very induftrioufly augmented them, by felling immenfe trees, and various other modes, that it was with the utmoft pains and fatigue we could work our way through them. Exclufive of thefe, the watery grounds and marfhes were fo numerous, that we were under the neceffity of conftructing no lefs than forty bridges to pafs them, and over one morafs there was a bridge of near two miles in length.

In our march through this wildernefs, as it may with propriety be called, we met with very little difficulty from the Americans. They fometimes, when our people were removing the obftructions we had continually to encounter, would attack them, but as they were only ftraggling

parties

parties, they were eafily repulfed. The diftance from our late encampment to this place was fmall, but the many obftacles the enemy had thrown in our way, made it a matter of aftonifhment, confidering the laborious march we had undergone, that we fhould arrive fo foon.

On our way, we marched acrofs the Pine-plains, which derive their name from an extenfive fpace of level country, on which grows nothing but very lofty pine-trees. On thefe plains we frequently met with the enemy's encampment, and about the center of them, upon fome rifing ground, there were exceeding ftrong works, defended by an immenfe abbatis, where it was thought they would wait our approach. But this pofition was not fuited to the Americans, for if their lines were forced, their rear was an open extent of country. It is a general obfervation, that they never make a ftand but upon an eminence, almoft

moft inacceffible, and a wood to cover their retreat.

At this encampment the expected Indians have joined us; they feem to poffefs more bravery, and much more humanity, than thofe who accompanied us acrofs Lake Champlain, as the following little anecdote will convince you:

A few days fince feveral of them fell in with a fcouting party of the Americans, and after a little fkirmifh, the enemy fled to their *batteaux*, and rowed acrofs the river. The Indians fired at, but could not reach them, and being greatly exafperated at their making their efcape, perceiving a hog-trough, they put their fire-arms into it, ftripped and fwam acrofs the river, pufhing the hog-trough before them. The Indians gained the fhore lower down than the Americans, furprized and took them prifoners.

prisoners, and brought them back in the *batteaux* acrofs the river.

One of the Americans, a very brave fellow, was wounded in the fkirmifh, and unable to walk, when the Indians brought him upon their backs for near three miles, with as much care and attention as if he had been one of their own people.

As the Indians approached the camp, we were all apprized of their bringing in fome prifoners, by their fetting up the war hoop; but every one was aftonifhed, and as equally pleafed at their humanity, in beholding an Indian bringing on his back the chief of the party. He was taken before General Frafer, but would give no anfwer to any queftion, and behaved in the moft undaunted manner. The General imagining that by fhewing him attention he might gain fome information from him, ordered him fome refrefhment,
and

and when the Surgeon had examined his wound, told him he muft immediately undergo an amputation, which being performed, he was requefted to keep himfelf ftill and quiet, or a locked jaw would inevitably enfue; to this he replied with great firmnefs, " then I fhall have the pleafure " of dying in a good caufe, that of gaining " independence to the American Colonies." I mention this circumftance, to fhew how chearfully fome of them will facrifice their lives in purfuit of this favorite idol. Such was the man's reftlefs difpofition, that he actually died the next morning. This death was generally regretted, as one among the very few who act from principle; had he furvived, a different ftatement of the cafe might have rendered him as ftrenuous a loyalift, as great a hero, as he was a ftubborn rebel.

To thofe who have been averfe to our employing Indians, a melancholy inftance
was

was lately afforded, that will afresh sharpen their arguments against the maxim, and as the matter will certainly be greatly exaggerated, when the accounts of it arrive in England, I shall relate to you the circumstance, as it really happened, and clearly point out the misfortune not to be the effect of their natural barbarity, but a disputed point of war.

A young lady, whose parents being well affected to Government, had abandoned their habitation to avoid the ill treatment of the Americans, and left their child alone in it, who, upon the approach of our army, was determined to leave her father's house and join it, as a young man, to whom she was on the point of being married, was an officer in the provincial troops. Some Indians, who were out upon a scout, by chance met with her in the woods; they at first treated her with every mark of civility they are capable of, and were conducting her into camp; when within a mile of it, a difpute arofe between the two Indians, whofe prifoner fhe was, and words growing very high, one of them, who was fearful of lofing the reward for bringing her fafe into camp, moft inhumanly ftruck his tomahawk into her fkull, and fhe inftantly expired.

The fituation of the General, whofe humanity was much fhocked at fuch an inftance of barbarity, was very diftreffing and critical; for however inclined he might be to punifh the offender, ftill it was hazarding the revenge of the Indians, whofe friendfhip he had to court, rather than to feek their enmity.

The Chief of the tribe to which the Indian belonged, readily confented to his being delivered up to the General, to act with him as he thought proper; but at the fame time faid, it was the rules of their

war,

war, that if two of them at the fame inftant feized a prifoner, and feemed to have an equal claim, in cafe any difpute arofe between them, they foon decided the conteft, for the unhappy caufe was fure to become a victim to their contention.

Thus fell a poor unfortunate young lady, whofe death muft be univerfally lamented. I am afraid you will accufe me of great apathy, and conclude the fcenes of war to have hardened my feelings, when I fay, that this circumftance, put in competition with all the horrors attendant on this unfortunate conteft, and which, in all probability, are likely to increafe hourly, is but of little moment.

The General fhewed great refentment to the Indians upon this occafion, and laid reftraints upon their difpofitions to commit other enormities. He was the more exafperated,

perated, as they were Indians of the remoter tribes who had been guilty of this offence, and whom he had been taught to look upon as more warlike. I believe, however, he has found equal depravity of principle reigns throughout the whole of them, and the only pre-eminence of the remoter tribes confifts in their ferocity.

From this time there was an apparent change in their tempers; their ill humor and mutinous difpofition ftrongly manifefted itfelf, when they found the plunder of the country was controuled; their interpreters, who had a *douceur* in the rapacity, being likewife debarred from thofe emoluments, were profligate enough to promote diffention, defertion and revolt.

In this inftance, however, *Monfieur St. Luc* is to be acquitted of thefe factions, though I believe he was but too fenfible of

their

their pining after the accuftomed horrors, and that they were become as impatient of his controul as of all other: however, thro' the pride and intereft of authority, and at the fame time the affectionate love he bore to his old affociates, he was induced to cover the real caufe under frivolous pretences of complaint.

On the 4th inftant, at the preffing inftance of the above gentleman, a council was called, when, to the General's great aftonifhment, thofe nations he had the direction of, declared their intention of returning home, at the fame time demanding the General to concur with and affift them. This event was extremely embarraffing, as it was giving up part of the force which had been obtained at a great expence to Government, and from whofe affiftance fo much was looked for: on the other hand, if a cordial reconciliation was made with them, it muft be by an indulgence in all their excesses of blood and rapine. Nevertheless the General was to give an immediate anfwer; he firmly refused their propofal, infifted upon their adherence to the reftraints that had been eftablifhed, and at the fame time, in a temperate manner, reprefented to them their ties of faith, of generofity and honor, adding many other perfuafive arguments, to encourage them in continuing their fervices.

This anfwer feemed to have fome weight with them, as many of the tribes neareft home only begged, that fome part of them might be permitted to return to their harveft, which was granted. Some of the remote tribes feemed to retract from their propofal, profeffing great zeal for the fervice.

Notwithftanding this, to the aftonifhment of the General, and every one belonging to the army, the defertion took
place

place the next day, when they went away by fcores, loaded with fuch plunder as they had collected, and have continued to do fo daily, till fcarce one of thofe that joined us at Skenefborough is left.

It is with great pleafure I acquaint you that Major Ackland is fo far recovered, as to affume his command of the grenadiers; he arrived at the camp yefterday, accompanied by the amiable Lady Harriet, who, in the opening of the campaign, was reftrained, by the pofitive injunction of her hufband, from fharing the fatigue and hazard that was expected before Ticonderoga. But fhe no fooner heard that the Major was wounded, than fhe croffed Lake *Champlain* to join him, determined to follow his fortunes the remainder of the campaign.

That your partner in the connubial ftate, fhould you be induced to change your

your situation, may prove as affectionate, and evince as tender an anxiety for your welfare, as Lady Harriet, on all occasions shews for that of the Major, is the ardent wish of

Yours, &c.

LETTER XXXVI.

Camp at Fort Edward, Aug. 8, 1777.

MY DEAR FRIEND,

WE ſtill remain at this encampment, till proviſions are brought up to enable us to move forward, and notwithſtanding theſe delays in our convoys and ſtores, it will certainly be thought we remain too long for an army whoſe buſineſs is to act offenſively, and whoſe firſt motion, according to the maxims of war, ſhould contribute, as ſoon as poſſible, to the execution of the intended expedition.

I know

I know it will be the general obfervation in England, that we ought, after we had penetrated thus far, to have made our way to Albany by rapid marches, it being no more than fifty miles diftant from this place. In this inftance it is to be confidered, how the troops are to pafs two great rivers, the Hudfon and the Mohawk, without *batteaux*; to form a bridge, or water-raft, to convey large bodies at once, even admitting the contrivance of a bridge of rafts to pafs the Hudfon, and truft to chance for the paffage of the Mohawk, or in cafe of a difappointment, recourfe to be had to the fords at *Schenectady*, which are fifteen miles from the mouth of the river, and are fordable; except after heavy rains: removing all thefe impediments, for a rapid march the foldier muft of courfe be exempted from all perfonal incumbrances, and reprefented as juft marching from a parade in England, for nothing can be more repugnant to the ideas of a rapid
march,

march, than the load a foldier generally carries during a campaign, confifting of a knapfack, a blanket, a haverfack that contains his provifion, a canteen for water, a hatchet, and a proportion of the equipage belonging to his tent; thefe articles, (and for fuch a march there cannot be lefs than four days provifion) added to his accoutrements, arms, and fixty rounds of ammunition, make an enormous bulk, weighing about fixty pounds. As the Germans muft be included in this rapid march, let me point out the incumbrance they are loaded with, exclufive of what I have already defcribed, efpecially their grenadiers, who have, in addition, a cap with a very heavy brafs front, a fword of an enormous fize, a canteen that cannot hold lefs than a gallon, and their coats very long fkirted. Picture to yourfelf a man in this fituation, and how extremely well calculated he is for a rapid march.

It

It may be urged, that the men might be relieved from a confiderable part of this burthen, and that they might march free from knapfacks and camp equipage, being divefted of which, they might have carried more provifion. Admitting this it would not remedy the evil, it being with great difficulty you can prevail on a common foldier to hufband his provifion, in any exigency whatever. Even in a fettled camp, a young foldier has very fhort fare on the fourth day after he receives his provifion; and on a march, in bad weather and bad roads, when the weary foot flips back at every ftep, and a curfe is provoked by the enormous weight that retards him, it muft be a very patient veteran, who has experienced much fcarcity and hunger, that is not tempted to throw the whole contents of his haverfack into the mire, inftances of which I faw on feveral of our marches. When they thought they fhould get frefh provifion

fion at the next encampment, and that only when they were loaded with four days provifion: the foldiers reafon in this manner: the load is a grievous incumbrance—want but a little way off—and I have often heard them exclaim, " Damn the provifions, we " fhall get more at the next encampment; " the General won't let his foldiers ftarve."

Confiftent with the idea of rapidity, it is neceffary to carry forward more provifion than for bare fuftenance during the march, or how were the men to fubfift when they arrived at Albany, where the Americans will certainly make a ftand? but even fuppofing they fhould not, they will of courfe drive off all the cattle, and deftroy the corn and corn-mills; this can only be effected by carts, which could not keep pace with the army, there being only one road from Albany for wheel-carriage, and in many places there are deep and wide
gullies,

gullies, where the bridges are broken, and muft neceffarily be repaired. This road is bounded on one fide by the river, and on the other by perpendicular afcents, covered with wood, where the enemy might not only greatly annoy, but where, in one night, they could throw impediments in our way, that would take nearly the whole of the next day to remove, therefore every idea of conveying more provifion than the men could carry on their backs muft ceafe, as the time and labor in removing thefe obftructions, and making new roads for the carts to pafs, before they could reach the army, would inevitably be the caufe of a famine, or the army muft retreat. All notion of artillery is totally laid afide, as in the prefent ftate of the roads, not the fmalleft ammunition tumbril could be carried with the army.

There are many who may be led away with the ideas of a rapid march, and fay
that

that artillery is ufelefs; but they can only form their opinion from the warmth of their wifhes. It is impoflible to judge, or form an opinion, unlefs upon the fpot, for, fpeaking within compafs, there are not lefs than a dozen ftrong paffes, fetting afide the paffage of the Mohawk; where, if ftrengthened with abbatis, which the Americans are expert in making, as they never encamped a fingle night without throwing up works of this fort in a few hours, five hundred of their militia would ftop, for a while, ten times their number of the braveft troops in the world, who had not artillery to affift them.

Having ftated thefe objections to the principles and practicability of a rapid march, you cannot but be fully convinced how neceffary it is to advance with a fufficient fupply of ftores, both of artillery and provifions; and in order to gain a great fupply

fupply of the latter, as well as to provide fome teams and oxen, a detachment is going to Bennington, to furprize a magazine of the enemy's, which will enable the army to proceed without delay, and its Commander to profecute the object of his expedition.

Certainly the fituation of the General is extremely trying, however zealoufly he is inclined, and anxious in compleating the object of his command. For one hour that he can devote in contemplating how to fight his army, he muft allot twenty to contrive how to feed it! This inconvenience the enemy have not to encounter, as their army is fpeedily and regularly fupplied with every thing, by means of their navigable rivers, which communicate from province to province. An American General has only to teach his men to fight, (that's a pretty difficult tafk you'll fay) he is never at a lofs how to feed them.

It

It is, from the various circumſtances I have ſtated, greatly to be wiſhed, that the minds of ſome men were more open to conviction, to form their opinions with the greater liberality of ſentiment.

A few days ſince I went from this to Fort George, relative to ſome artillery ſtores, at which place I had an opportunity of ſeeing Lake George, which, altho' confiderably ſmaller than Lake *Champlain*, in my opinion exceeds it far in point of beauty and diverſity of ſcene.

About the center of the lake there are two iſlands, on the largeſt of which, called Diamond Iſland, are encamped two companies of the 47th regiment, under the command of Captain Aubrey, for the purpoſe of forwarding the proviſions acroſs the lake. This iſland, as well as the one that is cloſe to it, formerly was ſo over-run with rattle-ſnakes, that perſons when they paſſed the lake feldom or ever ventured on them. A *batteaux* in failing up it, overfet near Diamond Ifland, and among other things it contained feveral hogs, which fwam to the fhore, as did the Canadians who were rowing it up : the latter, in apprehenfion of the rattle-fnakes, climbed up trees for the night, and the next morning obferving a *batteaux*, they hailed the people in it, who took them in and conveyed them to Fort George.

Some time after the man who owned the hogs, being unwilling to lofe them, returned down the lake, and with fome comrades ventured a fearch. After traverfing the ifland a confiderable time, they at laft found them, but fo prodigioufly fat, that they could fcarcely move, and in their fearch only met with one rattle-fnake, which greatly furprized them, as the ifland was reported to abound. Their wonder, however, was not of long duration, for being
fhort

short of provisions, they killed one of the hogs, the stomach of which was filled with rattle-snakes, and from this circumstance it was natural to conclude the hogs had devoured them since their landing.

This was related to me by a person on whose veracity I can depend, and several of the inhabitants have informed me since, that if a hog happens to meet a rattle-snake, it will immediately attack and devour it.

As I am on the subject of rattle-snakes, and this country greatly abounding with them, permit me to describe to you those reptiles, which I am the better enabled to do, having seen one killed yesterday. It was about a yard long, and about three inches in circumference, in its thickest part; it had seven rattles at the end of its tail, and according to the number of these rattles,

rattles, its age is afcertained, every year producing an additional one, fixed by a fmall ligament within the other, and being hollow, the quick motion of the tail occafions a noife fo peculiar to itfelf, that I cannot mention any thing fimilar to it. The fcales of thefe rattle-fnakes are of variegated colors, and extremely beautiful, the head is fmall, with a very quick and piercing eye; their flefh, notwithftanding the venom they are poffeffed of, is very delicious, far fuperior to that of an eel, and produces a very rich foup.

The bite of thefe reptiles is certain death, unlefs proper remedies are applied. Providence has been fo attentive to our prefervation (a pretty remark you'll fay this, to come from a foldier, who is contributing daily his affiftance to the deftroying and maiming hundreds), that near to where thefe reptiles refort, there grows a plant, with a large broad leaf, called *plaintain*,
which

which being bruised and applied to the wound, is a sure antidote to the ill effects of its venom. The virtues of this plant were discovered by a negro in Virginia, for which he obtained his liberty and a pension for life.

This discovery, like many others equally surprizing, was the mere effect of chance. This poor negro having been bit by one of these snakes, in the leg, it swelled in an instant to such a degree, that he was unable to walk; lying down on the grass in great anguish, he gathered some of this plant, and chewing it, applied it to the wound, imagining it would cool the inflammation; this giving him instant relief, he renewed the application several times, and the swelling abated, so as to enable him to walk home to his master's plantation; after repeating the same for the space of two or three days, he was perfectly recovered.

But however furrounded I may be with venomous reptiles, the clank of arms, and horrors of war, reft affured that neither diftance, time, nor place, can erafe the idea of friendfhip, nor the fweet thoughts of what is left behind ever be leffened in the breaft of

Yours, &c.

LETTER XXXVII.

Camp at Batten Kill, August 24, 1777.

MY DEAR FRIEND,

IT is with the utmost concern I tell you the expedition to Bennington has failed, and great numbers made prisoners: This no doubt will be a matter of great exultation to the Americans, and divest them of those fears they had entertained of the German troops, especially as they have been defeated by a set of raw militia. In this enterprize the General left nothing for chance to do, but planned every thing his wisdom could suggest to effect it, and the project would have answered many desirable defirable ends, had the execution of it proved as fortunate as the plan was judicious.

In some former letter I laid much stress against a rapid movement, and endeavored to point out to you the total impracticability of it. I need only add another argument to impress you fully with the same sentiments. The army could no more proceed without hospital stores, than it could without provisions, for depend upon it, the General who carries troops into fire, without precautions to alleviate the certain consequences, is sure to alienate their affections, and damp their ardor; it is exacting more than human spirit is able to sustain. It is not necessary for you to be accustomed to fields of battle, to be convinced of truth; let your mind only rest for a moment on the objects that present themselves after an action, and then reflect, there is not a mattrass for broken bones,

bones, nor a cordial for agony and faintnefs. Thofe whofe ideas are continually marching with a much greater rapidity than ever an army did, fuppofe no oppofition, and no fuffering from wounds. The many helplefs and in agonies, who muft be cruelly abandoned (fuppofing the reft could be prevailed on to abandon thofe whofe cafe might the next day be their own) make no confideration with men of precipitate imagination. I fhall clofe this fubject with obferving, that in my opinion, a General is refponfible to God and his country for the armies he conducts, and that he cannot eafily overlook thefe objects; however anxious he may be, he muft be patient till a few hundred beds, and a proper proportion of medicine and chirurgical materials, can be brought up for troops that are to *fight* as well as *march.*

In order to take advantage of the fuccefs that was expected from the expedition to Bennington, the army moved to the eaft fide of Hudfon's river, and on the 14th, a bridge of rafts was conftructed, over which the advanced corps paffed, and encamped on the heights at Saratoga.

Whatever was the caufe of the failure of the expedition to Bennington, of which many appear, the principal one feems to have been the delay of the reinforcement that was fent to fupport the firft detatchment, which was from eight o'clock in the morning to four o'clock in the afternoon of next day, marching two and twenty miles; the advanced corps, not only at the time the Germans were fent, but at the failure of it, felt themfelves much hurt, thinking it was a duty they ought to have been employed on, and it was not till after its failure, that impreffion was

erafed

erased from their minds, by being informed they were reserved for more important services; for in case that expedition had proved succesful, the advanced corps were to have pushed forward to the heights of Still-Water, and intrenched there till the army and provisions could have joined; by this means the whole country on the west side of the river to the banks of the Mohawk, would have been in our possession.

A few days after we had encamped at the heights of Saratoga, the bridge of rafts was carried away by the torrents occasioned by the late heavy fall of rain, and our communication cut off from the main body. If the enemy after the late successes, in our present situation, had been induced to attack us, the General would have found himself in a very bad position, and unable to take a better, as the advanced corps could not be supported by the line,

the

the only means of retreat would have been under the cover of our artillery, therefore our corps were recalled, after the action at Bennington, and were obliged to crofs the river in boats and fcowls, and take up our old encampment at this place.

The Mohawk nation, which are called Sir William Johnfon's Indians, as having their village near his plantation, and who, in his life-time, was continually amongſt them, were driven from their village by the Americans, and have joined our army: they have come with their *fquaws*, children, cattle, horfes and fheep, and are encamped at the creek from whence this place takes its name; when the army crofs the river, the *fquaws* and children are to go to Canada, and the men to remain.

Upon their arrival I vifited them at their encampment, and had an opportunity of obferving the mode they adopt in

training

training up their children. They are in a manner amphibious; there were several of the men bathing in the creek; and a number of little children, the eldeſt could not be more that ſix years old, and theſe little creatures had got into the middle of the creek upon planks, which they paddled along, ſometimes ſitting, then ſtanding on them, and if they overbalance the plank, and ſlip off with a dexterity almoſt incredible, they get on it again; as to diving, they will keep a conſiderable time under water, nearly two or three minutes.

The mode of confining their young infants, is by binding them flat on their backs to a board, and as they are ſwaddled up to their head, it makes them reſemble living mummies; this method of binding their young, I am led to imagine, is the cauſe of that perfect ſymmetry among the men. A deformed Indian is rare to be met with; the women would be be equally as perfect, but as they grow up, they acquire a habit, it being deemed an ornament, of so turning in the feet, that their toes almost meet; the *squaws*, after the have suckled their infants, if they fall asleep, lay them on the ground, if not they hang the board they are swaddled to on the branch of a tree, and swing them till they do; upon a march, they tie these boards, with their infants, on their backs.

As the river is subject to continual torrents and increase of water, a bridge of boats is now constructing, to preserve a communication with both sides of the river, which when compleated, the advanced corps are to pass over, and encamp at Saratoga.

I am interrupted by the cries of some Indians who are setting up the war whoop, on their bringing in prisoners. . . .

When

When they arrive, as they imagine, in hearing of the camp, they set up the war whoop, as many times as they have a number of prisoners. It is difficult to describe it to you, and the best idea that I can convey is, that it consists in the sound of *whoo, whoo, whoop!* which is continued till the breath is almost exhausted, and then broke off with a sudden elevation of voice; some of them modulate it into notes, by placing the hand before the mouth, but both are heard at a great distance.

Whenever they scalp, they seize the head of the disabled or dead enemy, and placing one of their feet on the neck, twist their left hand in the hair, by which means they extend the skin that covers the top of the head, and with the other hand draw their scalping knife from their breast, which is always kept in good order, for this cruel purpose, a few dextrous strokes of which takes off the part that is termed the
scalp;

scalp; they are so exceedingly expeditious in doing this, that it scarcely exceeds a minute. If the hair is short, and they have no purchase with their hand, they stoop, and with their teeth strip it off; when they have performed this part of their martial virtue, as soon as time permits, they tie with bark or deer's sinews their speaking trophies of blood in a small hoop, to preserve it from putrefaction, painting part of the scalp and the hoop all round with red. These they preserve as monuments of their prowess, and at the same time as proofs of the vengeance they have inflicted on their enemies.

At one of the Indian encampments, I saw several scalps hanging upon poles, in front of their *wigwams*; one of them had remarkably fine long hair hanging to it. An officer that was with me wanted to purchase it, at which the Indian seemed highly offended, nor would he part with
this

this barbarous trophy, although he was offered fo ftrong a temptation as a bottle of rum.

The appearance of a dead body, you muft allow, is not a pleafing fpectacle, but when fcalped it is fhocking; two, in this fituation, we met with, in our march from Skenefborough to Fort Edward. After fo cruel an operation, you could hardly fuppofe any one could furvive, but when we took poffeffion of Ticonderoga, we found two poor fellows who lay wounded, that had been fcalped in the fkirmifh the day before the Americans abandoned it, and who are in a fair way of recovery. I have feen a perfon who had been fcalped, and was as hearty as ever, but his hair never grew again.

Should I at any time be unfortunate enough to get wounded, and the Indians come acrofs me, with an intention to fcalp, it would be my wish to receive at once a *coup de grace* with their tomahawk, which in most instances they mercifully allow.

This instrument they make great use of in war, for in pursuing an enemy, if they find it impossible to come up with them, they with the utmost dexterity throw, and seldom fail striking it into the skull or back of those they pursue, by that means arresting them in flight. The tomahawk is nothing more than a small hatchet, having either a sharp spike, or a cup for tobacco, affixed opposite to the part that is intended for cutting, but they are mostly made to answer two purposes, that of a pipe and a hatchet. When they purchase them of the traders, they take off the wooden handle, and substitute in its stead a hollow cane one, which they do in a curious manner.

I make no doubt but it will afford you great pleasure, knowing how much you

are

are interefted in my welfare, when I inform you that I have had fome promotion, and it is the more fatisfactory to myfelf, as I am not removed out of the advanced corps, it being into the 24th regiment. If I efcape this campaign, either through intereft or purchafe, there are hopes of obtaining a company. With my beft wifhes for your health and happinefs, I am

Yours, &c.

LETTER XXXVIII.

Camp at Freeman's Farm, Sept. 24, 1777.

MY DEAR FRIEND,

THE bridge of boats was soon constructed, and thirty days provision brought up for the whole army. On the 13th instant, we passed Hudson's river, and encamped in the plains of Saratoga, at which place there is a handsome and commodious dwelling-house, with out-houses, an exceeding fine saw and grist-mill, and at a small distance a very neat church, with several houses round it, all of which are the property of General Schuyler. This beautiful spot was quite deserted,

not

not a living creature on it. On the grounds were great quantities of fine wheat, as alfo Indian corn; the former was inftantly cut down, threfhed, carried to the mill to be ground, and delivered to the men to fave our provifions; the latter was cut for forage for the horfes.

Thus a plantation, with large crops of feveral forts of grain, thriving and beautiful in the morning, was before night reduced to a fcene of diftrefs and poverty! What havoc and devaftation is attendant on war! Your coffee-houfe acquaintance, who fight battles over a bottle of wine, and dictate what armies fhould do, were danger only to fhew itfelf upon your coaft, and threaten an invafion, would inftantly, like the poffeffors of this delightful fpot, be flying to the moft interior parts of the kingdom.

On the 15th the whole army made a movement forward, and encamped at a place called *Dovacote*.

I omitted to mention a sad accident that happened to that amiable woman, Lady Harriet Ackland, a little before we passed Hudson's river, which neither has altered her resolution nor her chearfulness, but she continues her progress, partaking the fatigues of the advanced corps.

Our situation, as being the advanced post of the army, was frequently so very alert, that we seldom slept out of our cloaths. In one of these situations a tent, in which Major Ackland and Lady Harriet were asleep, suddenly caught fire; the Major's orderly serjeant, with great danger of suffocation, dragged out the first person he got hold of, which was the Major. It providentially happened, that in the same instant Lady Harriet, without knowing what

what she did, and perhaps not perfectly awake, made her escape, by creeping under the walls in the back part of the tent, and upon recovering her senses, conceive what her feelings must be, when the first object she beheld was the Major, in the midst of the flames, in search of her! The serjeant again saved him, but the Major's face and body was burnt in a very severe manner: every thing they had with them in the tent was consumed. This accident was occasioned by a favorite Newfoundland dog, who being very restless, overset a table on which a candle was burning, (the Major always had a light in his tent during the night, when our situation required it) and it rolling to the walls of the tent, instantly set them on fire.

On the 17th the army renewed their march, repairing a great number of bridges, and encamped on a very advantageous ground, at the distance of about four miles from

from the enemy, who are ftrongly pofted at Still-Water....

At our laft encampment a circumftance occurred, which though trifling in itfelf, marks how provident nature has been to the younger part of the brute creation. It is the cuftom in camp to picket the horfes in the rear of the tents: in the night I was awaked with a great ruftling of my tent cords, and a fqueaking noife; on getting up, I found it was a little colt that my mare had foaled. When we refumed our march the next day, I was much embarraffed what to do with the colt, fearful it would weaken my mare, and render her unable to convey my baggage, but I would not have it deftroyed; and, believe me, this little creature, only dropped the night before, though in a journey of fuch a diftance as feventeen miles, through thick woods and bad roads, was as gay and chearful, when we arrived at our encampment, as if it it had been in a meadow, after which, you may be fure, I could not find in my heart to make away with it.

On the 18th, the enemy appeared in force, to obftruct the men who were repairing the bridges, and it was imagined they had a defign of drawing us to action, in a fpot where artillery could not be employed; a fmall lofs was fuftained in fkirmifhing, and the repair of the bridges was effected.

At this encampment a number of men got into a potatoe-field, and whilft gathering them, a fcouting party of the enemy came acrofs and fired on them, killing and wounding near thirty, when they might with eafe have furrounded the whole party, and taken them prifoners. Such cruel and unjuftifiable conduct can have no good tendency, while it ferves greatly to increafe hatred, and a thirft for revenge.

On the 19th, the army marched to meet the enemy, in three divifions; the German line flanked the artillery and baggage, purfuing the courfe of the river through the meadows; the Britifh line marched parallel to it at fome diftance, through the woods, forming the center divifion; whilft the advanced corps, with the grenadiers and light infantry of the Germans made a large circuit through the woods, and compofed the right hand divifion; on our right there were flanking parties of Indians, Canadians and Provincials.

The fignal guns for all the columns to advance were fired between one and two o'clock, and after an hour's march, the advanced party, confifting of the picquets of the center column, under the command of Major Forbes, fell in with a confiderable body of the enemy, pofted in a houfe and behind fences, which they attacked, and after much firing, nearly drove in the

body

body of the Americans, but the woods being filled with men, much annoyed the picquets, who were very fortunately supported by two companies of the 24th regiment, one of which happened to be our company, and a piece of artillery, which General Frafer had detached, on hearing the fire of Major Forbes's party, and we came up juft as the enemy fled.

In this fkirmifh, a bat-man of General Frafer's refcued from the Indians an officer of the Americans, one Captain Van Swearingham, of Colonel Morgan's Virginia rifle-men; they were on the point of ftripping him, which the man prevented; and recovered his pocket-book from them, containing all his papers of confequence and his commiffion. He offered the foldier all his *paper* dollars, and lamented he had no *hard* ones to reward him with.

The

The bat-man brought him up to General Frafer (who now had come up to the two companies he had detached) when he interrogated him concerning the enemy, but could obtain no other anfwer, than that their army was commanded by Generals Gates and Arnold. General Frafer, exceedingly provoked that he could gain no intelligence, told him if he did not immediately inform him as to the exact fituation of the enemy, he would hang him him up directly; the officer, with the moft undaunted firmnefs, replied, " You may, " if you pleafe." The General perceiving he could make nothing of him, rode off, leaving him in the cuftody of Lieutenant Dunbar, of the artillery.

My fervant, juft at this period, arrived with my canteen, which was rather fortunate, as we ftood in need of fome refrefhment after our march through the woods,

woods, and this little fkirmifh. I requefted Dunbar, with his prifoner, to partake of it, and fitting down upon a tree, we afked this Captain a variety of queftions; to which he always gave evafive anfwers, and we both obferved he was in great fpirits: at laft I faid to him, "Captain, do you "think we fhall have any more work upon "our hands to day?" to which he replied, "Yes, yes, you'll have bufinefs enough, "for there are many hundreds all round "you now." He had hardly fpoke the words, when from a wood a little way in our front there came an exceffive heavy fire. Dunbar ran to his guns, faying A——, you muft take charge of the Captain. There being only one officer, befides myfelf, with the company, I committed him to the cuftody of a ferjeant, to convey him to the houfe where the reft of the prifoners were, with particular orders, as the General had defired, that he fhould not be ill treated; I then haftened to my company,

company, on joining of which I met a number of the men who were retiring wounded, and by this time the firing of the enemy was fuppreffed by the artillery.

Shortly after this we heard a moſt tremendous firing upon our left, where we were attacked in great force, and the very firſt fire, your old friend, Lieutenant Don, of the 21ſt regiment, received a ball through his heart. I am fure it will never be erafed it from my memory; for when he was wounded, he fprung from the ground, nearly as high as a man. The party that had attacked us were again drove in by our cannon, but the fire raged moſt furiouſly on our left, and the enemy were marching to turn their right flank, when they met the advanced corps, poſted in a wood, who repulfed them. From that time, which was about three o'clock, till after fun-fet, the enemy, who were continually fupplied with freſh troops,
moſt

moſt vigorouſly attacked the Britiſh line: the ſtreſs lay upon the 20th, 21ſt, and 62d regiments, moſt part of which were engaged for near four hours, without intermiſſion. The grenadiers and 24th regiment, as well as part of the light infantry, were at times engaged. In the conflict the advanced corps could only act partially and occaſionally, as it was deemed unadviſeable to evacuate the heights where they were advantageouſly poſted.

General Phillips, at a very critical period, when the Britiſh line was hard preſſed, by a great ſuperiority of fire, brought up four pieces of artillery, which reſtored the action, and gallantly led up to the 20th regiment, at the utmoſt hazard of his perſon.

General Reideſel exerted himſelf, brought up the Germans, and arrived in time to charge the enemy with great bravery.

Juſt

Juſt as the evening cloſed in, the enemy gave way one all ſides and left us maſters of the field, but darkneſs prevented a purſuit.

The troops lay that night upon their arms, and the next day took a poſition nearly within cannon-ſhot of the enemy; we have fortified our right, and our left extends to the brow of the heights, ſo as to cover the meadows, by the river ſide, where the *batteaux* and hoſpitals are placed. The 47th regiment, with the regiments of *Heſſe Hanau*, are encamped in the meadows, as a farther ſecurity.

The great valor diſplayed by the Britiſh troops encountering many obſtructions, and ſuch a powerful enemy, as, from the account of the priſoners, they had nearly treble our numbers in the field, and the great advantage of receiving inſtant reinforcements, muſt, in the eyes of thoſe who

who judge impartially, reflect the highest honor.

Notwithstanding the glory of the day remains on our side, I am fearful the real advantages resulting from this hard-fought battle, will rest on that of the Americans, our army being so much weakened by this engagement, as not to be of sufficient strength to venture forth and improve the victory, which may, in the end, put a stop to our intended expedition; the only apparent benefit gained, is that we keep possession of the ground where the engagement began.

This severe-fought battle, and the consequences resulting from it, will fully confirm the arguments I pointed out to you relative to a rapid march. The victory must inevitably have been on the side of the Americans, without our artillery, and what a wretched state must the many brave soldiers

soldiers be in, without any comfort, or an hospital to remove them to!

The courage and obstinacy with which the Americans fought, were the astonishment of every one, and we now become fully convinced, they are not that contemptible enemy we had hitherto imagined them, incapable of standing a regular engagement, and that they would only fight behind strong and powerful works.

We have lost many brave men, and among that number is to be lamented Captain Jones, of the artillery, who was killed at his brigade of guns. The artillery of the army distinguished themselves greatly, but this brigade in particular, the officers and men stationed at those guns being all killed and wounded, except Lieutenant Hadden, who had a very narrow escape, his cap being shot away as he was spiking up the cannon.

Having

Having juft received orders to attend a working-party, to throw up a redoubt, I am obliged to defer a further account of this engagement till my next. It will no doubt afford you much pleafure to hear, that in this fevere action I have efcaped unhurt.

Yours, &c.

LETTER XXXIX.

Camp at Freeman's Farm, Oct. 6, 1777.

MY DEAR FRIEND,

WE have gained little more by our victory than honor, the Americans working with inceſſant labor to ſtrengthen their left; their right is already unattackable. Inſtead of a diſheartened and flying enemy, we have to encounter a numerous, and, as we lately experienced, a reſolute one, equally diſpoſed to maintain their ground as ourſelves, and commanded by Generals whoſe activity leave no advantages unimproved.

The

The day after our late engagement, I had as unpleasant a duty as can fall to the lot of an officer, the command of the party sent out to bury the dead and bring in the wounded, and as we encamped on the spot where the three British regiments had been engaged, they were very numerous. In a former letter I described to you the sensations both before and after a battle, but in such an employment, as this the feelings are roused to the utmost pitch. You that are pleased to compliment me on my humanity, will think what I must have felt, on seeing fifteen, sixteen, and twenty buried in one hole. I however observed a little more decency than some parties had done, who left heads, legs and arms above ground. No other distinction is paid to officer or soldier, than that the officers are put in a hole by themselves. Our army abounded with young officers, in the subaltern line, and in the course of this unpleasant duty, three of the 20th regiment were interred together, the age of the eldeſt not exceeding ſeventeen. This friendly office to the dead, though it greatly affects the feelings, was nothing to the ſcene in bringing in the wounded; the one were paſt all pain, the other in the moſt excruciating torments, ſending forth dreadful groans. They had remained out all night, and from the loſs of blood and want of nouriſhment, were upon the point of expiring with faintneſs: ſome of them begged they might lay and die, others again were inſenſible, ſome upon the leaſt movement were put in the moſt horrid tortures, and all had near a mile to be conveyed to the hoſpitals; others at their laſt gaſp, who for want of our timely aſſiſtance muſt have inevitably expired. Theſe poor creatures, periſhing with cold and weltering in their blood, diſplayed ſuch a ſcene, it muſt be a heart of adamant that could not be affected at it, even to a degree of weakneſs.

In

In the courfe of the laft action, Lieutenant Hervey, of the 62d, a youth of fixteen, and nephew to the Adjutant-General of the fame name, received feveral wounds, and was repeatedly ordered off the field by Colonel Anftruther; but his heroic ardor would not allow him to quit the battle, while he could ftand and fee his brave lads fighting befide him. A ball ftriking one of his legs, his removal became abfolutely neceffary, and while they were conveying him away, another wounded him mortally. In this fituation the Surgeon recommended him to take a powerful dofe of opium, to avoid a feven or eight hours life of moft exquifite torture: this he immediately confented to, and when the Colonel entered the tent with Major Harnage, who were both wounded, they afked whether he had any affairs they could fettle for him? his reply was, " that being a minor, every " thing was already adjufted;" but he had one requeft, which he had juft life enough

to utter, " Tell my uncle I died like a fol-
" dier!" Where will you find in ancient
Rome heroifm fuperior!

Beyond the ground where we defeated
our enemy, all is hoftile and dangerous in
an alarming degree; it fhould feem as if we
had conquered only to preferve our reputation, for we have reaped little advantage
from our invincible efforts ; the only fatis-
faction refulting on our part is, the con-
fcioufnefs of having acquitted ourfelves
like men, with a determination that the
honor and renown of the Britifh arms
fhould remain unfullied. The nature of
the country is peculiarly unfavorable in refpect to military operations, it being difficult to reconnoitre the enemy, and to obtain any intelligence to be relied on: the
roads, the fituation of the enemy, the
grounds for procuring forage, of which
the army is in great want, and all parties
are in queft of, are often attended with the
utmoft

utmoſt danger, and require great bodies to cover them.

The expectation of plunder which had induced the Indians that remained to accompany us thus far, beginning now to fail, and ſeeing they have nothing but hardſhips and warfare, they are daily decreaſing. They were of vaſt ſervice in foraging and ſcouting parties, it being ſuited to their manner; they will not ſtand a regular engagement, either through the motives I formerly aſſigned, or from fear, but I am led to imagine the latter is the caſe, from the obſervation I have made of them in our late encounter with the enemy. The Indians were running from wood to wood, and juſt as our regiment had formed in the ſkirts of one, ſeveral of them came up, and by their ſigns were converſing about the ſevere fire on our right. Soon after the enemy attacked us, and the very firſt fire the Indians run off through the wood.

As

As to the Canadians, little was to be depended on their adherence, being eafily difpirited, with an inclination to quit as foon as there was an appearance of danger; nor was the fidelity of the Provincials to be relied on who had joined our army, as they withdrew on perceiving the refiftance of the Americans would be more formidable than had been expected.

The defertion of the Indians, Canadians, and Provincials, at a time when their fervices were moft required, was exceedingly mortifying; and however it may prove, this inftance, will fhew future commanders what little dependence is to be placed on fuch auxiliaries.

You will readily allow that it is the higheft teft of affection in a woman, to fhare with her hufband the toils and hardfhips of the campaign, efpecially fuch an one as the prefent. What a trial of
fortitude

fortitude the late action must have been, through a distressing interval of long suspence! The ladies followed the route of the artillery and baggage, and when the action began, the Baroness Reidesel, Lady Harriet Ackland, and the wives of Major Harnage and Lieutenant Reynell, of the 62d regiment, entered a small uninhabited hut, but when the action became general and bloody, the Surgeons took possession of it, being the most convenient for the first care of the wounded; in this situation were these ladies four hours together, when the comfort they afforded each other was broke in upon, by Major Harnage being brought in to the Surgeons deeply wounded! What a blow must the next intelligence be, that informed them Lieutenant Reynell was killed! Madame de Reidesel and Lady Harriet could afford but little consolation to their companions, through an anxiousness they knew not how to smother, lest it might be soon,

very

very foon, their own fituation. The fears of Lady Harriet were doubly increafed, having every apprehenfion, not only for her hufband but her brother.

Surrounded by the dead and the dying for four long hours, the groans of the wounded, the difcharge of the mufquetry, and all the buftle of arms—my God!— what a ftate for women of fufceptibility! —uncertain how the battle would terminate, and whether each fhould clafp again the object of her deareft hopes, for whofe fake fhe had traverfed dreary regions, encountered hunger and wearinefs, and witneffed all the carnage of a long-difputed field—unanimated by the tumult, and without fharing the glory.

A long war teaches the moft unwarlike nation the ufe of arms, and very frequently puts them in a condition to repair in the end, the loffes they fuftained in the beginning.

beginning. Such is the prefent ftate of the enemy, who not only now, but before the late action, were ftrongly recruited, as powerful armies of militia fpring up in every province. What a ftriking advantage there was on the fide of the Americans, in the laft engagement; but the defect of numbers in our little army, was amply made up by the courage of the foldiers, the valor and conduct of our Generals.

The officers who have been killed and wounded in the late action, are much greater in proportion than that of the foldiers, which muft be attributed to the great execution of the rifle-men, who directed their fire againft them in particular; in every interval of fmoke, they were fure to take off fome, as the rifle-men had pofted themfelves in high trees. Some of the prifoners who were taken late in the day, faid, it was firmly believed in the enemy's enemy's camp, that General Burgoyne was killed, which miftake was occafioned by an Aid-de-Camp of General Phillips, a Captain Green, who, having the furniture to his faddle laced and embroidered, and being wounded, fell from his horfe, the rifle-man that wounded him, from that circumftance, affirmed it to be General Burgoyne.

You would be led to imagine, that the Indians and Canadians would have been of great utility againft this mode of fighting, but the few who remained of the former, could not be brought within found of a rifle-fhot; and the latter, who formerly were very expert in this fervice, either from a great change in their military character, or a damp that was thrown upon them by the lofs of their beft officers, who were under the neceffity of expofing themfelves more than was requifite, in order to bring them at all into action, were of little ufe.

Some

Some of the Provincial troops were serviceable, but the only men we had really to oppose them were the German chaffeurs, but their number was very inferior to the rifle-men of the enemy.

Our present situation is far from being an inactive one, the armies being so near, that not a night passes but there is firing, and continual attacks upon the advanced picquets, especially those of the Germans. It seems to be the plan of the enemy to harrass us by constant attacks, which they are enabled to do, without fatiguing their army, from the great superiority of their numbers.

We are now become so habituated to fire, that the soldiers seem to be indifferent to it, and eat and sleep when it is very near them; the officers rest in their cloaths, and the field officers are up frequently in the night. The enemy, in front of our quarter

ter-guard, within hearing, are cutting trees and making works, and when I have had this guard, I have been vifited by moft of the field officers, to liften to them. You would fcarcely believe it, but the enemy had the affurance to bring down a fmall piece of cannon, to fire as their morning gun, fo near to our quarter-guard, that the wadding rebounded againft the works.

We have within thefe few evenings, exclufive of other alarms, been under arms moft of the night, as there has been a great noife, like the howling of dogs, upon the right of our encampment; it was imagined the enemy fet it up to deceive us, while they were meditating fome attack. The two firft nights this noife was heard, General Frafer thought it to have been the dogs belonging to the officers, and an order was given for the dogs to be confined within the tents; any that were feen running about, the Prevoft had orders to hang them.

The

The next night the noise was much greater, when a detachment of Canadians and Provincials were sent out to reconnoitre, and it proved to have arisen from large droves of wolves that came after the dead bodies: they were similar to a pack of hounds, for one setting up a cry, they all joined, and when they approached a corpse, their noise was hideous till they had scratched it up.

I have sent you a view of the encampment of our hospital tents, park of artillery, &c. from a redoubt we have on the opposite side of the river, by which you may be able to form some idea of the country we are at present encamped on. This view was taken by Sir Francis Clerke, one of General Burgoyne's Aid-de-Camps, who has favored me with a copy.

Yours, &c.

LETTER XL.

Cambridge, in New England, Nov. 10, 1777.

MY DEAR FRIEND,

THE difpatches fent by Lord Peterfham, relative to our misfortunes, will have reached England long before this comes to hand. Your furprize, then, will ceafe at receiving a letter dated from this place. As every little circumftance relative to a campaign, cannot be given in an official account to be laid before the public, I fhall relate the tranfactions of the army till the convention took place.

The day after the date of my laſt letter, a detachment of 1500 regular troops, with two twelve-pounders, two howitzers, and ſix ſix-pounders, went out between eleven and twelve o'clock. The reaſon, no doubt, for the General's marching at this time, rather than earlier in the morning, was, that in caſe we ſhould not prove victorious, he had the night to favor his retreat.

The intention of this detachment was to make a movement to the enemy's left, not only to diſcover whether there was a poſſibility of forcing a paſſage, if neceſſary to advance, or diſlodge the enemy, in order to favor a retreat, but likewiſe to cover the forage of the army, through the ſcarcity of which we were in great diſtreſs. This being a project of much importance, General Burgoyne took with him Generals Phillips, Reideſel and Fraſer, as officers beſt qualified, and with whoſe aſſiſtance he had every hope the plan would ſucceed.

The guard of the camp upon the heights was left to the command of Brigadier Generals Hamilton and Specht, and the redoubts and plain to Brigadier General Gall.

This day having the quarter-guard of the regiment, I of courfe remained in camp, and therefore can give you no information as to the various pofitions that were taken; after the detachment had been out fome time, we heard a very heavy firing with the artillery, and fome little fkirmifhing with fmall arms.

At this time Major Campbell, of the 29th regiment, the Field-officer of the day, came to my guard, and defired me to go with a ferjeant and fome men, to reconnoitre acrofs two ravines, in front of the guard, to liften if I could hear the enemy marching that way; all was quiet in that quarter, but as the firing began to be very heavy

heavy on the left, I returned to the guard. In this little circuit I was convinced how much the Americans were pushed in our late action, on the 19th of September, for I met with several dead bodies belonging to the enemy, and amongst them were laying close to each other, two men and a woman, the latter of whom had her arms extended, and her hands grasping cartridges.

Soon after my return to the guard, the firing appeared to become general on both sides, and very heavy indeed. Much about this time the bat-men of the army, who went out for forage, came galloping into camp, having thrown off their forage to save their own horses and themselves by flight. The gallant behaviour of an old soldier, of the 20th regiment, deserves to be remembered; he had been wounded at the battle of Minden, and as he lay on the ground a French dragoon rode over him,

and

and the horfe's feet refted on his breaft; after having recovered from this accident, he thought himfelf invulnerable, and held the Americans in great contempt: when they attacked the foraging party, the hardy old veteran, fitting upon the forage which he had got on the horfe, kept loading and firing his piece at the enemy, and in this manner he brought his forage into camp. Upon his arrival, his mafter reprimanded him for the danger he had expofed both himfelf and his horfes to, (when he faid) "May it pleafe your honor, "I could not throw away my forage, I'd "fooner lofe my life, than my poor horfes "fhould ftarve."

You muft allow this defeat of the batmen, and a number of wounded men coming into camp, was no very favorable omen of fuccefs; nor can you conceive the forrow vifible on General Frafer's being

brought

brought in wounded, your old friends Campbell and Johnston, of our regiment, on each fide of his horfe, fupporting him. I cannot defcribe to you the fcene; it was fuch that the imagination muft help to paint.——The officers, all anxious and eagerly enquiring as to his wound—the down-caft look and melancholy that was vifible to every one, as to his fituation, and all the anfwer he could make to the many enquiries, was a fhake of his head, expreffive that it was all over with him.— So much was he beloved, that not only officers and foldiers, but all the women flocked round, folicitous for his fate.

When he had reached his tent, and was recovered a little from the faintnefs occafioned by lofs of blood, he told thofe around him, that he faw the man who fhot him, he was a rifle-man, and up in a tree; the ball entered a little below his breaft, breast, and penetrated juft below the back bone. After the Surgeon had dreffed his wound, he faid to him very compofedly, "Tell me, Sone, to the, beft of your fkill and judgment, if you think my wound is mortal." When he replied, " I am forry, Sir, to inform you, that it is, and that you cannot poffibly live four and twenty hours." He then called for pen and ink, and after making his will, and diftributing a few little tokens of regard to the officers of his fuite, defired that he might be removed to the general hofpital.

In camp, and not in perfonal danger, as the mind is left to reflection, it is impoffible to defcribe how much it is affected in beholding the wounded continually coming in, amid an inceffant roar of cannon and mufquetry, where perhaps many brave fellows are dying for their country—perhaps too

too in an unfuccefsful battle! I can never confent to be left in camp again.

After many hours impatient anxiety, towards the clofe of the evening, the grand ftroke came. I had little hope to become a partaker in the action; but about that time the troops came pouring into camp as faft as they could, and fhortly after Generals Burgoyne, Phillips and Reidefel. It is impoffible to defcribe the anxioufnefs depicted in the countenance of General Burgoyne, who immediately rode up to the quarter-guards, and when he came to that of our regiment, I was acrofs a ravine, pofting a ferjeant's guard. Upon enquiring eagerly for the officer, I came to him, " Sir, faid the General, you muft defend " this poft to the very laft man." You may eafily conceive, upon receiving thofe orders, I judged every thing to be in a dangerous fituation. There was not a moment for thought, for the Americans
ftormed

ſtormed with great fury the poſt of the light-infantry, under the command of Lord Balcarres, ruſhing cloſe to the lines, under a ſevere fire of grape-ſhot and ſmall arms. This poſt was defended with great ſpirit, and the enemy, led on by General Arnold, as gallantly aſſaulted the works; but on the General's being wounded, the enemy were repulſed, which was not till after dark. In this attack, I was but an obſerver, as our quarter-guard was ſome diſtance from the lines, but not ſufficiently ſo as to be out of danger, as the balls were continually dropping down amongſt us. In order that you may form ſome idea with what obſtinacy the enemy aſſaulted the lines, from the commencement, at which time it was dark, till they were repulſed, there was a continual ſheet of fire along the lines, and in this attack we were fully convinced of what eſſential ſervice our artillery was.

During

During the time the enemy were so
vigorously attacking our lines, a party
assaulted those of the Germans, commanded by Colonel Breyman, but either
for want of courage, or presence of mind,
they, upon the first attack of the enemy,
were struck with such a terror, that instead of gallantly sustaining their lines, they
looked on all as lost, and after firing one
volley, hastily abandoned them; that brave
officer, Colonel Breyman, in endeavouring
to rally his soldiers, was unfortunately
killed. By the enemy's obtaining possession
of the German lines, they gained an
opening upon our right and rear.

In this engagement we lost many brave
officers, to add to the fate of General
Fraser, General Burgoyne's, Aid-de-Camp,
Sir Francis Clerke, was killed, Colonel
Ackland wounded and a prisoner, Major
Williams, Captain Blomfield, and Lieutenant Howarth, of the artillery, were
likewise

likewise prisoners, the latter wounded; Major Blomfield's wound was very remarkable, a shot passing through both cheeks, without hurting the inside of his mouth. Your friend Howarth's wound I hear, is in his knee; it is very singular, but he was prepossessed with an idea of being wounded, for when the orders came for the detachment's going out, he was playing picquet with me, and after reading the orders, and that his brigade of guns were to go, he said to me, " God bless you " A——, farewell, for I know not how it " is, but I have strange *presentiment* that I " shall either be killed or wounded." I was rather surprized at such an expression, as he is of a gay and chearful disposition, and cannot but say, that during the little time I could bestow in reflection that day, I continually dwelt upon his remark, but he is now happily in a fair way of recovery.

After

After Major Ackland was wounded, when he obferved the army were retreating, he requefted Captain Simpfon, of the 31ft regiment, who was an intimate friend, to help him into camp, upon which, being a very ftout man, he conveyed the Major on his back a confiderable way, when the enemy purfuing fo rapidly, he was obliged to leave him behind to fave himfelf. As the Major lay on the ground, he cried out to the men who were running by him, that he would give fifty guineas to any foldier who would convey him into camp. A ftout grenadier inftantly took him on his back, and was haftening into camp, when they were overtaken by the enemy and made prifoners. Here you muft naturally conceive what were the feelings of Lady Harriet, who, after hearing the whole of the action, at laft received the fhock of her individual misfortune, mixed with the general calamity of the defeat.

Whatever

Whatever favorable opinion the General had entertained of our late encampment, after this attack he thought our flank liable to be turned, and it would be impoffible to accomplifh an honorable retreat, fearing the only fecurity of the army would confift in an ignominious flight, as our works would by no means refift cannon-fhot. Before we quitted them, we heard the enemy bringing up their artillery, no doubt with a view to attack us at daybreak; therefore, laboring under thefe apparent difadvantages, we had orders to quit our prefent fituation during the night, and take poft upon the heights, above the hofpital; by this movement the whole of the army were now affembled upon the heights and plain, of which you have a view in the drawing I fent you.

Our late movement, which was effected without any lofs, occafioned the enemy to make a new difpofition, and on the

the 8th of October, the baggage and incumbrances of the army being removed, we offered battle, anxious for a conflict in a plain, where we could discern our enemy, as hitherto all our actions had been in the woods, where it is impossible exactly to prescribe to an army, or separate body, how to govern itself; every different motion of the enemy, and the various accounts a General receives of them, ought to make him alter his measures, and there is no laying down to a commanding officer of any corps, other than general rules, the rest depending on his own conduct, and the behaviour of his troops.

At one time we fully imagined it was the intention of the enemy to have attacked us, as a very large body, consisting of several brigades, drew up in line of battle, with artillery; and began to cannonade us. In return, an howitzer was fired, and, as was intended, the shell fell short,

short, upon which the enemy setting up a great shout, were very much encouraged, and kept on cannonading. The next time the howitzer was so elevated, that the shell fell into the very center of a large column, and immediately burst, which so dismayed them, that they fled off into the woods, and shewed no other intentions of an attack; indeed their cautious conduct during the whole day strongly marked a disinclination to a general action.

Early on this morning General Fraser breathed his last, and at his particular request, was buried, without any parade, in the great redoubt, by the soldiers of his own corps. About sun-set, the corpse was carried up the hill; the procession was in view of both armies; as it passed by Generals Burgoyne, Phillips and Reidesel, they were struck at the plain simplicity of the parade, being only attended by the officers of his suite; but left the army,

not

not being acquainted with the privacy that was defired, and conftrue it into neglect, and urged by a natural wifh to pay the laft honors to him, in the eyes of the whole army, they joined the proceffion.

The enemy, with an inhumanity peculiar to Americans, cannonaded the proceffion as it paffed, and during the fervice over the grave. The account given me by your friend Lieut. Freeman was, that there appeared an expreffive mixture of fenfibility and indignation upon every countenance— the fcene muft have been affecting.

In the evening intelligence was brought that the enemy were marching to turn our right; we could prevent this by no other means than retreating towards Saratoga. A retreat is a matter of the higheft confequence, and requires the greateft conduct in a General, as well as refolution in both officers and foldiers, for the leaft mifma- nagement

nagement puts all into confusion. A good retreat is looked on as the *chef d'œuvre* of a Commander. Every one of the advanced corps felt feverely the loss of General Fraser, as he used frequently to say, that if the army had the misfortune to retreat, he would ensure, with the advanced corps, to bring it off in safety; this was a piece of Generalship he was not a little vain of, for during the war in Germany, he made good his retreat with five hundred chasseurs, in fight of the French army. But as covering the retreat of the army was of the utmost consequence, General Phillips took the command of the rear-guard, which consisted of the advanced corps.

. At nine o'clock at night the army began to move, General Reidesel commanding the van-guard. Our retreat was made within musquet-shot of the enemy, and though greatly encumbered with baggage, without

without a single loss. It was near eleven o'clock before the rear-guard marched, and for near an hour, we every moment expected to be attacked, for the enemy had formed on the same spot as in the morning; we could discern this by the lanterns that the officers had in their hands, and their riding about in the front of their line, but though the Americans put their army in motion that night, they did not pursue us, in our retreat, till late the next day. Deferring the sequel of our misfortunes till another opportunity, and willing to embrace a very favorable one that now presents itself of sending this, I remain,

Yours, &c.

LETTER XLI.

Cambridge, in New England Nov. 15, 1777.

MY DEAR FRIEND,

AFTER a march, in which we were
liable to be attacked in front, flank
and rear, the army, on the 9th, at day-
break, reached an advantageous ground,
and took a position very desirable to
have received the enemy; we halted to refresh the troops, and to give time for
the *batteaux* to come abreast of the army.
A few days provision was delivered out,
and it was apprehended it might be the last,
for though the movement of the army kept
pace with the *batteaux*, still there were
many

many parts of the river where they might have been attacked to great advantage, and where the army could afford them little protection.

After the troops had been refreshed, and the *batteaux* came up, the army proceeded forward, in very severe weather, and thro' exceeding bad roads, and late at night arrived at Saratoga, in such a state of fatigue, that the men had not strength or inclination to cut wood and make fires, but rather sought sleep in their wet cloaths and on the wet ground, under a heavy rain that still continued, and which began to fall when we first retreated.

The incessant rain during our retreat was rather a favorable circumstance, for though it impeded the army in their march, and increased its difficulties, it served at the same time to retard, and in a great measure prevented, the pursuit of the enemy;

it

it however occafioned one very unhappy neceffity, that of abandoning our hofpitals with the fick and wounded: but great praife is due to the humanity of General Gates, for upon the very firft intelligence of it, he immediately fent forward a few light horfe, to protect them from infult and plunder.

The heavy rain afforded another confolation to the men during the march, which was, in cafe the enemy had attacked us, the fate of the day would have refted folely upon the bayonet: this idea prevailed fo ftrongly in the minds of the men, that notwithftanding they were acquainted with the fuperiority of the enemy, an attack feemed to be the wifh of every foldier.

When the army were about to move after we halted, the cares and anxieties with which the General, no doubt, muft have been furrounded, were greatly increafed

creafed by a circumftance of private diftrefs, for at this time a meffage was delivered to him from that amiable woman, Lady Harriet Ackland, expreffing an earneft defire, if it did not militate againft the General's wifhes, of paffing to the camp of the enemy, and requefting General Gates's permiffion to attend her hufband, at the fame time fubmitting it entirely to the General's opinion.

The General, although he had been fully convinced of the patience and fortitude with which fhe had already encountered the many trying fituations that had befallen her, could not but exprefs his aftonifhment at this propofal, as it appeared an effort beyond human nature, that a woman of fuch a tender and delicate frame as her's, fhould be capable of fuch an undertaking as that of delivering herfelf to the enemy—probaby in the night, and uncertain of what hands fhe might fall into—

efpecially

especially after so long an agitation of the spirits, not only exhausted by want of rest, but absolutely want of food, and drenched in rains for near twelve hours—and this at a time too, when far advanced in a state where every tender care and precaution becomes absolutely requisite!——In the harrassed and fatigued situation she was in, it was no little chagrin to the General, that he could afford her no assistance to cheer up her spirits for such an undertaking; he had not even a cup of wine to offer her— but from a soldier's wife she obtained a little rum and dirty water! With this poor refreshment she set out in an open boat, which was furnished by the General, with a few lines of recommendation to General Gates, for his protection. The Chaplain that officiated at General Frafer's funeral undertook to accompany her, and with her waiting-maid, and the Major's *valet de chambre* (who then had a ball in his shoulder, which he received in the late action,

in

in fearching for the Major after he was wounded) fhe rowed down the river to meet the enemy.——But to return to the army.

It was not till after day-light, on the morning of the 10th, that the artillery and the laft of the troops paffed the Fifh-Kill, and took pofition upon the heights and in the redoubts we had formerly conftructed. On our arrival at Saratoga, a corps of the enemy, between five and fix hundred, were difcovered throwing up intrenchments on the heights, but upon our approach retired over the ford of the Hudfon's river, and joined a body pofted to oppofe our paffage there.

A detachment of artificers, under a ftrong efcort, were fent to repair bridges, and open a road on the weft fide of the river to Fort Edward; but the enemy being ftrongly pofted on the heights of the Fifh-Kill,

Kill, and making a difposition to give us battle, that efcort was recalled. The Provincials who were left to cover the artificers, upon a very flight attack ran away, leaving them to efcape as they could, without a poffibility of their performing any work.

While thefe different movements were carrying on, the *batteaux* with provifions were frequently fired upon from the oppofite fide of the river, fome of them were loft, and feveral men killed and wounded in thofe that remained.

On the 11th the enemy continued the attacks upon the *batteaux*, feveral were taken and retaken, but their fituation being nearer to the main force of the enemy than to ours, it was judged neceffary to land the provifions, and fend them up the hill, as it was impoffible to fecure them by any other means: this was effected

under

under a heavy fire, and with the greateft
difficulty.

The intentions of the enemy became now very apparent, and no doubt General Gates thought he fhould be able to gain more advantage from the fituation and circumftances of our army, by cutting off our provifions, and otherwife harraffing and diftreffing us, by the galling fire of the riflemen, who were every where placed about in the woods, than by giving us battle, and running the chance of a victory.

The poffible means of farther retreat were confidered in a council of war, compofed of the General officers; and the only one that feemed expedient, or in the leaft practicable, was attended with fuch danger, as afforded little hopes of fuccefs, but neverthelefs the refolve was it fhould be attempted. This was by a night march to Fort Edward,

ward, the troops carrying their proviſions on their backs, leaving artillery, baggage, and other incumbrances behind, and to force a paſſage at the ford, either above or below that fort.

While the army were preparing for this bold and reſolute undertaking, ſome ſcouts returned with intelligence, that the enemy were ſtrongly intrenched oppoſite thoſe fords, and poſſeſſed a camp in force on the high grounds, between Fort Edward and Fort George, with cannon; excluſive of which, they had parties down the whole ſhore to watch our motions, and ſome poſts ſo near us, on our ſide of the water, that it was impoſſible the army could make the leaſt motion without being diſcovered.

Notwithſtanding the number of the Americans, which was hourly increaſing, General Gates acted with as much precaution as if the ſuperiority was on our ſide,

as

as the ground where he encamped was, from its nature and the works he had thrown up, inattackable.

Our march to Fort Edward being thus prevented, the army was pofted as well as the ground would admit of, fortifying our camp, and preparing for any attempt that the enemy, from our reduced ftate, might be induced to make.

The ftate and fituation of our army was truly calamitous!—Worn down by a feries of inceffant toils and ftubborn actions; abandoned in our utmoft diftrefs by the Indians; weakened by the defertion, and difappointed as to the efficacy of the Canadians and Provincials, by their timidity; the regular troops reduced, by the late heavy loffes of many of our beft men and diftinguifhed officers, to only 3500 effective men, of which number there were not quite 2000 Britifh:—in this ftate of weaknefs ness, no possibility of retreat, our provisions nearly exhausted, and invested by an army of four times our number, that almost encircled us, who would not attack us from a knowledge of our situation, and whose works could not be assaulted in any part. In this perilous situation the men lay continually upon their arms, the enemy incessantly cannonading us, and their rifle and cannon shot reaching every part of our camp.

True courage submits with great difficulty to despair, and in the midst of all those dangers and arduous trials, the valor and constancy of the British troops were astonishing: they still retained their spirits, in hopes that either the long-expected relief would arrive from New-York, which the army implicitly believed, from an order that had been given out at our camp at Still-Water, stating that powerful armies were to act in co-operation with

with ours, or that the enemy would attack us, which was moſt fervently wiſhed for, as it would have given us an opportunity of dying gallantly, or extricating ourſelves with honor.

After waiting the whole of the 13th day of October, in anxious expectation of what it would produce, and to which time it had been reſolved to endure all extremities in maintaining our ground againſt the enemy—no proſpect of aſſiſtance appearing, and no rational ground of hope remaining, it was thought proper, in the evening, to take an exact account of the proviſions left, which amounted to no more than three days ſhort allowance.

In this ſtate of diſtreſs, a council of war was called, to which all the Generals, Field-officers, and commanding-officers of corps were ſummoned, when it was unanimouſly agreed, that in the preſent circumſtances

we

we could do no other than treat with the enemy.

Overtures were accordingly propofed to General Gates, who harfhly rejected them, reminding us of our enervated ftate, from a toilfome campaign, diminifhed numbers, fcanty fubfiftence, and the impoffibility of frefh fupply. Thefe reafons were urged on the fpur of the moment, minute confideration denied, and a decifive anfwer required. We felt their force, but compliance was never thought of, it would have too feverely wounded the dignity of our military character.

The refufal of our overtures was mortifying in the extreme, yet inftead of depreffing, it raifed our magnanimity; the interval of fufpence, indeed, difturbed our repofe; anxiety was awake to confequences—ftill we adhered to our purpofe with manly firmnefs. A ftate of fufpence, to a reflecting

ing mind, is worfe than death; that was our ftate till the convention was finally adjufted.

The obftacles to the accomplifhment of the convention at firft appeared infurmountable, for General Gates conceived that our complicated embarraffments fufficiently juftified him, according to the rules of war, in infifting on an unconditional furrender of the army: they were difdainfully rejected, and he was peremptorily informed, that notwithftanding our reduced numbers, if he ftill perfifted, our final appeal fhould be to the fword, as the Britifh troops would rufh upon the enemy, determined to give no quarter.

General Gates, from having been once in our fervice, was fully convinced of what exertions Britifh troops were capable, in any dangerous emergency; he was therefore quickly fenfible of the impolicy of
coercion,

coercion, and with very great prudence declined hazarding a fresh conflict with men who preferred death to a disgraceful submission. Awed by our firmness, he retracted his demands, and honorable terms were granted; the particulars, as they are undoubtedly in the Gazette, I shall of course pass over.

To a reverse of fortune we yielded with becoming dignity, but our honor was safe, and equanimity of temper marked our character, even in adversity.

General Burgoyne has done every thing in this convention for the good of the troops, consistent with the service of his King and country: all that wisdom, valor, and a strict sense of honor could suggest. Confident, no doubt, of having exerted himself with indefatigable spirit in their service, he will despise popular clamor, truly sensible that no perfect and unbiassed judge

of

of actual service can condemn him. Addison has somewhere observed,

" 'Tis not in mortals to command success!"

And as the populace, in this versatile age startle at untoward events, so our General is liable to be exposed to public censure. Ample justice must raise him in the mind of every liberal man who will judge with caution, acquit him with honor, and take him to his heart as the soldier's friend——as a man of cool judgment, but ardent for glory.——as courageous but unfortunate!

END OF THE FIRST VOLUME.

www.ingramcontent.com/pod-product-compliance
Lightning Source LLC
Chambersburg PA
CBHW051159300426
44116CB00006B/374